A Short History of Irel

A Short History of Ireland

From earliest times to the present day

J. C. Beckett

**Formerly Professor of Irish History
Queen's University of Belfast**

οἰκέομεν δ' ἀπάνευθε πολυκλύστῳ ἐνὶ πόντῳ
ἔσχατοι

Hutchinson of London

Hutchinson & Co. (Publishers) Ltd
3 Fitzroy Square, London W1P 6JD

London Melbourne Sydney Auckland
Wellington Johannesburg and agencies
throughout the world

First published 1952
Second edition 1958
Reprinted 1961, 1964
Third edition 1966
Reprinted 1967, 1968, 1969
Fourth edition 1971
Fifth edition 1973
Reprinted 1975, 1977
Sixth edition 1979
© J. C. Beckett 1952, 1958, 1966, 1971, 1973, 1979

Printed in Great Britain by The Anchor Press Ltd
and bound by Wm Brendon & Son Ltd
both of Tiptree, Essex

ISBN 0 09 139840 1 cased
     0 09 139841 X paper

Contents

Maps

Preface to the first edition

The task of writing a general history is almost bound to be a thankless one. Selection and compression are its necessary foundations, and both expose the writer to criticism. No two historians will agree on what should be excluded, and it is hard to compress without either obscuring or over-simplifying the issue. To such criticism there is no answer; for no one is more acutely aware than the writer himself how much has been left out and how imperfect is his exposition of what remains. But after all it is idle to blame a small book for not being a big one; as Dr Johnson said, 'All claret would be port if it could.'

Within the narrow space at my disposal I have traced the historical background of the two states of contemporary Ireland. I have no theory to vindicate, no policy to defend. I am concerned only to disentangle a confused stream of events and to make the present situation intelligible by showing how it arose. To this end I have thrown most weight on the modern period, and this has involved some concentration on Anglo-Irish relations. This concentration is not unreasonable, for English influence has been the strongest and most continuous force in the development of our political institutions and our economic life. At the same time, Irish history is not just a department of the history of England. The 'English in Ireland', like the institutions they brought with them, were modified by trans-plantation, and even when they clung to a connection upon which they believed their political and economic security to depend they continued to regard themselves as Irishmen. For this reason I have refused to define the term 'Irish' in any narrow racial or linguistic sense, and have tried to write a history of the whole country.

The task has been made easier by the great development of Irish historical studies which has taken place during the last fifteen years and which has contributed to a broader and more unified under-standing of Ireland's past. Whatever merit this book may possess as a new presentation of Irish history is due very largely to the work of others, but I am particularly indebted to Professor G. O. Sayles of Queen's University, Belfast; Dr R. B. McDowell of Trinity College, Dublin; Mr David Kennedy, MSC; and Dr J. L. McCracken, all of whom read portions of the book in typescript and gave me the advantage of their criticism and advice. Mr J. L. Lord, MA, read the entire work in proof and made many valuable suggestions. My thanks are also due to Sir Maurice Powicke, the editor of the series, for his help and encouragement. It should perhaps be added that I myself am wholly responsible for the opinions expressed in this book and for any errors that it may contain.

Preface to the sixth edition

It is now close on thirty years since this book was written. During that period research in Irish history has made considerable progress. I have endeavoured to incorporate the results in this new edition, as far as the limits of space allow. In particular, recent work on social and economic conditions in the eighteenth and nineteenth centuries has shown that long-accepted views are no longer tenable; and the relevant sections have been extensively rewritten. I have also taken this opportunity to revise and rearrange the list of further reading so as to make it more useful both to the general reader and to the student.

The historian's concern is with the past rather than with the present. The significance of the events and developments that he seeks to interpret can be judged only in retrospect; and the nearer he approaches the contemporary scene the more uncertain must his interpretation become. For this reason, I have chosen 1972, which marked the breakdown of constitutional arrangements made fifty years earlier, as a terminal point; but in the epilogue I have offered a brief and tentative assessment of the new situation thus created.

1 Ancient and medieval

Ireland before the Normans

Irish history, like the history of other countries, has been strongly influenced by geographical factors. For many centuries Ireland lay outside the main current of European life, but her insular position and comparative remoteness gave no lasting protection against invasion. An island people without command of the sea was easily open to attack, and Ireland's broad, slow-moving rivers offered convenient access from the coast to the interior. But isolation had its effects. Immigrants with their backs to the sea mingled readily with the preceding population, and the people of Ireland today are remarkably homogeneous in their physical characteristics. Though the interior can be reached easily from the coast, Ireland has no natural focal point, no great crossing-place of routes, no centre from which influence spreads naturally to the circumference. This was one of the factors which helped to prevent the establishment of political unity from within. Dublin is essentially an invaders' capital; founded originally by the Norsemen it became the centre of Anglo-Norman power in Ireland chiefly because of its position on the east coast, within easy reach of the ports of Bristol and Chester. This brings us to the most significant factor in the political geography of Ireland, the position of Great Britain as a barrier between Ireland and the continent. In historical times almost every important influence which has reached Ireland from the continent has been filtered through Great Britain. Today, when English political power has receded, English influence remains predominant in many spheres of life. The very fact that English remains the language of the vast majority of Irishmen has far-reaching effects on education, on literary activity and on popular taste; and it is hardly less important that Ireland remains a country of the common law. The close connection between the two islands, which has been a basic factor in Irish history, still remains, even though its character has changed.

The ancient Gaelic writers carry the history of Ireland as far back as Noah's flood; modern archaeologists find traces of human occupation for many thousands of years before Christ; but the cautious historian has to be content with a more recent beginning. The Gaels, or Goidels (with whom this beginning can best be made), probably reached Ireland during the first century BC, coming directly from Gaul. They found Ireland already occupied by a mixture of peoples, the descendants of earlier invaders from Great Britain and the continent, and some at least of these peoples probably spoke a Celtic dialect similar to Gaelic. The Gaels treated the existing population in much the same way as they themselves were to be treated by later invaders: they killed some, dispossessed others and compelled the rest to pay tribute. In spite of their iron weapons they made a very slow conquest and the pre-Gaelic population, especially in the north, long retained its independence. The epic poem *Táin Bó Cualgne* (The cattle-raid of Cooley) tells how the 'men of Ulster' led by Connor Mac Nessa and the Red Branch Knights, aided by the heroic Cuchulain ('the hound of Ulster'), defended the north against the 'men of Ireland', led by Queen Maeve. The details are legendary, but the general theme represents an historical reality.

Even when the Gaelic conquest was complete, which cannot have been before the fifth century AD, the Gaels formed only a dominant minority, an ascendancy class, holding the best land and trying to concentrate political power in their own hands. Though there was a steady mingling of population, the formal distinction between 'free' and 'tributary' tribes remained until the twelfth century. But long before this the Gaels had imposed their language and their legal system upon the whole country, and Gaelic historians and genealogists had reconstructed the past so as to obscure the great diversity in the origins of the population.

On the continent the Gaels had been organized in aristocratic republics, but in Ireland they adopted monarchical government. To begin with, there was no idea of a united monarchy for the whole island. Instead, there grew up a vast number of tiny states, each governed by a king or chief elected by the freemen from among the members of a ruling family. The boundaries of these states were ill-defined, for the king's authority was personal rather than territorial. These small states naturally tended to form into groups, each dominated by one relatively powerful ruling family, and this process was aided by the traditional division of the country which the Gaels found on their arrival – the 'five fifths of Ireland'. In fact, it does not appear that this fivefold division ever existed in historical times; but by the fifth century there were seven 'provincial kings', each ruling directly a small state of his own and exercising an external supremacy over a group of other similar states. The political pattern was logically completed by a 'high king' (*árd rí*), himself ruling a province and exercising supremacy over the other provincial kings. But this is a comparatively late development; it was probably not until the fifth century that a claim to such a general superiority was first put forward by the kings of Tara. Even when a high king had secured general recognition by making 'the circuit of Ireland' and exacting hostages from the provincial kings his authority was little more than nominal. The condition of Ireland at this time resembled in some ways that of ancient Greece: there was no effective political unity, but there was a cultural unity based on language, religion and law. Like other Celtic-speaking peoples the Gaels practised a form of Druidism, and this was common to the whole country; but while Ireland remained comparatively isolated, the sharp contrast with the foreigner, which is needed to give such community its full significance, was lacking. In theory, the legal system should have been a more effective bond. It was built up on collections of rights and precedents recorded and interpreted by the 'brehons', a class of professional lawyers, from whom the whole is usually called the 'brehon law'. But this law had no regular sanctions; the brehons were arbitrators rather than judges and their decisions could be enforced only by private action or public opinion.

For many centuries after the Gaelic invasion Ireland remained comparatively isolated. The Romans made no attempt at conquest, and though there was some intercourse with Britain and the continent, the Irish were outside the main stream of European development. When they do appear, at the end of the fourth century and the beginning of the fifth, it is among the barbarians whose savage raids helped to break down the declining Roman civilization of Britain. In one of these raids a Christian boy of sixteen, a Roman citizen, Patrick by name, was carried off to Ireland as a slave. A few years later he escaped, and after studying in Gaul and being consecrated bishop, he returned to Ireland to preach the Gospel. According to traditional account, St Patrick landed in County Down in 432 and died in 465, and within that relatively brief period traversed almost the whole country, establishing churches and appointing bishops and priests. Modern scholars query these dates and confine the personal exertions of Patrick to a relatively small area. But the fact remains that before his mission the Christians in Ireland were few and scattered, with no ecclesiastical organization and no bishop; after it the church was firmly established, and paganism, though still strong, was on the decline. And all this seems to have been accomplished peacefully; early Christian Ireland has no recorded martyrs.

From the beginning, Irish Christianity developed characteristics of its own. Elsewhere, the church was being built up in lands which had once formed part of the Roman empire, where the tradition of territorial divisions was strongly established; the word 'diocese' was itself taken over from the Roman administrative system. But in Ireland territorial divisions were of secondary importance; the unit of government was an amalgamation of kinship groups dominated by a ruling family, and church organization followed a similar pattern; the country was not cut up into dioceses, but bishops were attached to particular families. Their great number (Patrick is said to have appointed 300 of them) and the nature of their position prevented them from developing the kind of authority wielded by bishops on the continent. The typical religious centre in early Christian Ireland was not an episcopal see, but a monastery. An Irish monastery did not consist of a compact group of stone buildings. It was a little town of wooden huts, laid out in streets and grouped round a small stone church. Here hundreds of monks lived and worked and prayed together under the rule of an abbot, who was usually elected from among the family of the founder. These and other peculiarities of the Irish church were accentuated by the fact that the political condition of Europe during the centuries which followed the downfall of the western empire made regular communication between Ireland and Rome difficult.

Almost at the same time as Patrick and his successors were establishing Christianity in Ireland the Anglo-Saxon invaders were destroying it throughout a great part of Britain. The British church, which had never been strong or adventurous, made little effort to evangelize them, and the work of recovering the lands lost to Christianity was first undertaken by Irish missionaries. One of the earliest and most famous was St Columba of Derry who founded the monastery of Iona in 563, and from there much of southern Scotland and northern England was evangelized during the next hundred years. Other Irish saints carried on the work not only in Britain but on the continent: St Columbanus in Burgundy and Italy, St Kilian in Saxony, St Fiachra and St Fursa in Gaul, St Livinius in the Netherlands. Wherever they went these saints founded monasteries:

Lindisfarne, St Gall, Bobbio, are perhaps the most famous links in a chain which stretched from the British Isles to Italy.

These saints and monasteries were noted for educational as well as for religious zeal. In pre-Christian times the professional scholar had had an honoured place in Irish life and this tradition continued. Though St Patrick himself was not a man of great learning, he had brought Ireland into touch with Roman civilization before it had been almost completely overthrown by the barbarian invasions of the fifth and sixth centuries. Ireland herself escaped these invasions and so was able to act as guardian and transmitter of much that might otherwise have been destroyed. The Irish monastic schools, partly on account of their learning, partly because of their peaceful seclusion, attracted many scholars from abroad. As teachers, as scribes and as commentators Irish monks rendered great service to Europe, and the revival of learning under Charlemagne owes an incalculable debt to their work and inspiration.

During the sixth, seventh and eighth centuries Ireland was free from invasion; but internal warfare continued. The introduction of Christianity helped to strengthen the cultural links between one kingdom and another, but did little to promote political unity. When, after a long respite, Ireland fell victim to a new wave of barbarian attacks from the north, the country was unable to offer united resistance.

In Ireland as elsewhere in western Europe the Norse attacks began with scattered raids for booty, which were followed by permanent settlements and systematic efforts at conquest. By the middle of the ninth century Norse galleys had passed up the Bann to Lough Neagh and up the Shannon to the central plain; Norse city states, the first real cities in Ireland, had been founded at Dublin, Wexford, Waterford, Cork, Limerick. The struggle continued with varying fortunes throughout the ninth and tenth centuries and reached its climax in 1014 in a battle fought at Clontarf, on the outskirts of Dublin. Here Brian Boru, the *árd rí*, defeated a Norse alliance, drawn from the Orkneys, the Hebrides and Man, as well as from the settlements in Ireland, though at the cost of his own life. 'Brian's battle', as the sagas call it, was one of the bloodiest of the age; it was a great blow to Norse power and a final check to any attempt at a Norse conquest of Ireland

The magnitude of this victory and the fact that it was won by an *árd rí* must not be allowed to hide the fact that there was little unity among the Irish kings, who were often ready to use the Norse as allies in their wars with one another. Even at Clontarf the Irish of Leinster fought against Brian because they resented his attempt to destroy their independence. In England the Danish invasions had so weakened Northumbria and Mercia that the way was prepared for national unity under Wessex; but in Ireland the provincial kingdoms and provincial rivalries survived. This stands out quite clearly in Brian's own career. In the 970s he had established himself against various rivals as king of Cashel, with supremacy over Munster. He was now determined to secure the high kingship, which for five centuries had been confined to the *Uí Néill*, the descendants of the famous fourth-century king, Niall of the Nine Hostages. The high king of the time, Malachy II, was waging successful war against the Norsemen of Dublin; but Brian did not hesitate to attack him, and sent the Norse galleys of Limerick up the Shannon to ravage the lands of Malachy and his allies in Connaught and Meath. In 1002 Malachy was induced to give way and Brian took the high kingship. The chronicles speak of this as a 'usurpation', and though Brian did something to justify his act by trying to make the office effective, and though his proud description of himself as 'emperor of the Irish' was not entirely an empty boast, he accomplished little towards turning Ireland into a national state. Even the army with which he won his great victory was drawn almost entirely from the south. With his death all the old internal struggles broke out afresh; Malachy resumed the high kingship and Brian's successors had to fight to maintain even the supremacy he had won in Munster.

It is natural to think of the Norse invasions as a period of destruction and tyranny. But the Norsemen contributed much of value to the life of the country, for they were traders as well as robbers. It was they who first established town life in Ireland, and these towns were centres of peaceful commerce as well as of more violent undertakings; their ships carried the hides and wool of Ireland to Britain and Europe and brought back wine and cloth and slaves. This town life was scarcely affected by Brian's victory of Clontarf, for the Irish army was too weak to take Dublin or any of the other Norse strongholds. Indeed, the Irish had no desire either to expel the Norsemen or to occupy their towns, and though from time to time the settlers were obliged to recognize the overlordship of some Irish king, they remained as self-governing communities, known as 'Ostmen' (or 'easterners'). The Ostmen soon became Christian, and intermarried frequently with the Irish, but they remained a distinct people; those of Dublin, for example, had a bishop of their own who was subject to Canterbury, and not, like the Irish bishops, to Armagh.

This continued independence of the Norse cities was due at least in part to the break-down of the high kingship. For more than 150 years after Brian's death it was the prize of contending dynasties – O'Brien of Munster, Mac Lochlainn of Ulster, O'Connor of Connaught. Some sort of succession was maintained; but the kings were, as the chroniclers say, 'kings with opposition', exercising little authority outside their own provinces except what they could temporarily enforce by superior strength. Though the long-drawn-out struggle was probably bringing the country nearer to effective unity, the process was a slow one. But we must not exaggerate the impact of recurrent warfare on everyday life. The campaigning season was short; the forces engaged were rarely large; and it is safe to assume that much of the fighting recorded by the chroniclers hardly disturbed the bulk of the population.

The ecclesiastical developments of this period were more decisive than the political. The Irish church had been greatly weakened by the Norse wars, the peaceful life of the monasteries had been broken up and religion and learning had suffered as a result. There had been some recovery, especially in Munster, under Brian's vigorous rule; but the remoteness of Ireland, once a protection, was now a clog on progress. Ireland, 'a kingdom apart by herself', had little share in the intellectual ferment of the twelfth-century renaissance. At the same time the wider contacts being made through the Norse towns revealed to Irish churchmen the full extent of their divergence from the rest of western Christendom. By the middle of the twelfth century some progress had been made towards reform. A territorial diocesan system was established, and the dioceses were grouped in four provinces under the archbishops of Armagh, Dublin, Cashel and Tuam; each of the four archbishops received his *pallium* from the pope, thus formally recognizing his dependence upon Rome. About the same time Cistercian monks were introduced, and monasteries in the European style began to replace the old Irish foundations. Much of this reform was due to the efforts of St Malachy; in 1139 he visited Rome on behalf of the Irish bishops; in 1148 he set out on a second visit, but died on the way, at St Bernard's monastery of Clairvaux. Bernard's biography of Malachy shows what an unfavourable impression of the Irish church Malachy's account of it had created; and it was in order to promote the work of reformation that the papacy urged upon Henry II of England the duty of conquering the country and conferred upon him the title 'Lord of Ireland'. But Henry, his hands already full with the management of his scattered and troublesome empire, rejected the proposal; and it was not until many years later, when Ireland offered a potential threat to his security, that he was willing to intervene in its affairs.

The circumstances that brought Henry to Ireland have their origin within the country itself. In the struggle for the high kingship Dermot MacMurrough, king of Leinster, had supported the Mac Lochlainn claim. Consequently, when Rory O'Connor of Connaught seized power in 1166 Dermot found his position threatened. He resolved to seek help abroad, and obtained from Henry II permission to enlist allies among the marcher lords of south Wales, a mixed breed of Normans, Flemings and Welsh. Their mail-clad soldiers, their archers, their skill in fortification, were too much for the Irish, and with their help Dermot speedily recovered his kingdom. The most important of these auxiliaries was Richard de Clare ('Strongbow'), to whom Dermot gave his daughter Eva in marriage, and with her the promise of succession to the kingdom of Leinster. This promise was of no force in Irish law, but when in 1171 Dermot died, Strongbow seized and held Leinster, including the all-important city of Dublin, despite the opposition of the high king and of the Ostmen.

It was at this point that Henry II himself intervened. He came with a considerable army, not to conquer Ireland, but to make sure that his powerful barons did not establish independent Irish principalities. He asserted his authority over all the lands that had been occupied, and though Strongbow received a grant of Leinster, and Hugh de Lacy of Meath, they were to hold their lands as the king's tenants. The Norse towns, which were of vital military and economic importance, were not included in the grants but were retained by the king in his own immediate control. As for the native Irish rulers, most of them were quite willing to recognize Henry as their overlord. They were alarmed at the military strength of the invaders, and hoped that submission to Henry would protect them from attack; besides this, Henry was known to have the backing of the papacy and he was welcomed by the clergy, especially by the reformers, who looked to him for support. A national synod was held at Cashel, by Henry's direction, and decreed many reforms, of which the general effect was to bring the Irish church into line with the English. Thus, amid the general approval of ecclesiastical and secular powers, Henry II established the 'lordship of Ireland', which was to last for almost four centuries, until another Henry turned it into a kingdom.

The lordship of Ireland

The arrival of Henry II opened a new phase in Anglo-Irish relations; but it is misleading to regard the events of these years as constituting an 'English conquest' of Ireland. The invaders were Norman, Norman-Welsh and Flemish, rather than English, and their language and traditions were French. Though Henry II was king of England the Irish rulers submitted to him personally, not to the English crown. He simply added Ireland to the many other dominions which he ruled under various titles and by various rights. The fact that a few years later Henry transferred the lordship of Ireland to his younger son John, at a time when it was by no means certain that John would succeed to the throne of England, shows that he did not regard the political union between the two islands as indissoluble.

Henry's brief visit to Ireland had been sufficient for his immediate purpose; but many questions remained unsettled, especially that of the constitutional relationship between the lord of Ireland and the Irish kings. None of them had resisted, but many, including the *árd rí* Rory O'Connor, had made no formal submission, and until he at least had recognized Henry's overlordship there could be no hope of establishing political stability. The church was particularly anxious for a settlement, and Laurence O'Toole, archbishop of Dublin, was one of those mainly responsible for bringing about the treaty of Windsor between Henry and Rory in 1175. By this treaty Rory recognized Henry as his overlord and in return was confirmed in his kingdom of Connaught 'as fully and as peacefully as he held it before the lord king entered Ireland' on payment of an annual tribute of hides. Rory's position as *árd rí* was also recognized and he was to be responsible for collecting from the other Irish kings the tribute due to Henry; but his control was not to extend over the territories 'which the lord king has retained in his lordship and in the lordship of his barons'. At the time of the treaty, these territories comprised the former Irish kingdoms of Leinster and Meath, and the Norse cities and kingdoms of Dublin, Wexford and Waterford.

The system of dual government which the treaty of Windsor professed to set up never worked and never could have worked. Rory's high-kingship had been resisted even before the invasion, and now it was little more than an empty claim; he was in no position to exact tribute on Henry's behalf from other Irish kings and there is no evidence that he ever tried to do so. Whatever supremacy or central authority now existed was vested in the lord of Ireland, and Rory O'Connor had no successor as *árd rí*.

This was not the only element of unreality in the treaty. Henry had promised, at least by implication, to respect Irish territories beyond the boundaries of Leinster and Meath; but he found it impossible to restrain the land-hunger of the barons already settled in Ireland and of those who followed within the next few years. He had confirmed Strongbow in possession of Leinster and had granted Meath to Hugh de Lacy. In spite of some local Irish resistance the two earls rapidly developed their territories: they carved them up into manors, established sub-tenants, built castles, founded abbeys, granted charters to towns and, in general, reproduced the whole framework of feudal society. Their success was infectious, and other men pressed on into Irish territory. To some of them Henry was induced to make grants, despite the treaty of Windsor; but some of them acted independently, and the king had no effective means of controlling them, or of protecting the rights of Irish rulers who had accepted his supremacy. This expansion did not follow any plan. Individual leaders pursued their own interests and established their own claims as best they could. Their successes were due to their courage and energy and to the superior equipment of their forces. Frequently, also, they were aided by divisions among the Irish. In one native kingdom after another disputed successions and rival ambitions opened the way for intervention, and intervention was followed by conquest. It was by playing on such differences that the Normans gradually established themselves in Munster and in Connaught. In the north the Irish showed an unusual degree of unity, and yet it was here that Norman daring won its most spectacular victory. In 1177 John de Courcy, with a band of some 300 followers, invaded the kingdom of Ulidia, overthrew the combined forces of the northern kings, and established his rule from Carlingford Lough to Fair Head. Later tradition speaks of him as 'earl of Ulster', but there is no trace of any royal grant; to his contemporaries he was simply 'Conquestor Ultoniae', holding by the right of his sword. In both titles there was an implicit claim to the whole northern province; but in fact neither de Courcy nor his successors extended their power west of Lough Neagh and the river Bann.

It was by local and independent exploits of this kind that Norman power spread over Ireland during the fifty or sixty years which followed the first invasion. Such a piecemeal conquest was very different from Norman policy in England a century earlier, when the whole country had been systematically and speedily subjugated. This difference arose from a radical difference in circumstances. William's governing purpose was to conquer England and make it the effective centre of his power, while Henry's intervention in Ireland had been little more than incidental, a response to a potential threat. Besides this, the England to which William came had already achieved some degree of unity and possessed a working administrative system that he could take over and adapt. But in Ireland there was no central government for Henry to take over; and Irish and feudal law were so far apart as to make amalgamation impossible without radical changes on one side or the other. It is significant that whereas William had promised to govern England according to the laws of Edward the Confessor, Henry did not – indeed could not – give any corresponding promise in Ireland: the main reason for his coming, the establishment of Strongbow in Leinster, was itself a defiance of the Irish law of succession.

Henry's intervention had succeeded in its primary purpose – to prevent the emergence of an independent Norman power on his western flank; but if success were to be permanent he must establish and maintain an effective royal administration in Ireland; and this proved a more difficult task. The king was represented in Ireland by a 'justiciar' (as he was in England also during his absences from that country), but Henry's jealousy of the magnates made him unwilling to entrust any one of them with the office for more than a brief period. The transfer of the lordship to John may have been partly intended to improve the situation, but it had little effect, for John was a boy of ten at the time, and even after he reached maturity he paid only one brief visit to Ireland before his accession to the English throne in 1199. The feudal basis on which the conquered territory had been settled had, however, necessarily carried with it some framework of government. The tenants-in-chief formed a council upon which the justiciar could call for advice, though not for assistance in the day-to-day work of administration, and the collection of money payments due from them to their overlord involved the establishment of some sort of exchequer. Besides this, the division of Leinster, Meath, 'Ulster' and other lands among sub-tenants meant the setting up of seignorial courts administering feudal law. But there was no royal justice in Ireland until King John established a justiciar's court, which later developed into the court of King's Bench in Ireland. The appointment of an itinerant judge about the same time marked another step towards reproducing in Ireland the contemporary English judicial system.

In 1210 John came to Ireland again. His main object was to curb the power of the barons, for Ireland, like the Welsh marches, threatened to become a centre of baronial resistance to the crown and a refuge for rebellious vassals. He brought with him a considerable army; and though he remained only two months he marched through a great part of the country, from Waterford to Carrickfergus, westwards almost to the Shannon and east again to Dublin, reasserting royal authority throughout the whole area of Norman settlement. Though he did not do all that tradition has ascribed to him in the way of establishing counties, setting up law courts and building castles, he did leave the Dublin government more effective than he found it. Before his departure he compelled the magnates to swear that they would observe in Ireland the laws and customs of England. No doubt this general extension of English law to Ireland was meant to apply, at least in the first instance, only to the Norman settlers, but it involved the whole problem of future relations with the native Irish. If there was to be, in the long run, a real unification of the country, then the English legal system must be universally applied; if, on the other hand, the king's justice was to be confined to his Norman subjects, then the latter would remain a colony, surrounded by an alien and probably hostile population. The problem was not a simple one. Even within the area over which the invaders were generally dominant there remained large districts under the effective control of Irish kings, vassal states rather than integral parts of the lordship. The application to them of English law would involve a complete overthrow of their existing social system. In areas where English law prevailed the barons tended to treat the native Irish as *betaghs* (serfs or villeins); and in Ireland, as throughout feudal Europe, the serf was excluded from the royal courts. But some native Irish families were admitted to the benefit of English law; and if the authority of the lordship had been directly effective over the whole country the way would have been open for the establishment of a single legal system applying equally to all. But though, for a time, Norman power continued to expand, it was later halted and turned back; and the area within which the royal courts could function regularly shrank to little more than a narrow coastal strip.

John's example in visiting Ireland was not followed by any English king until Richard II came over in 1394, and this absenteeism made the maintenance of a strong central government more difficult. The weakness of feudalism everywhere was that the force of royal justice depended mainly on the vigour and ability of the king, and if royal justice was weak the barons were almost compelled to settle their differences by war. This is what happened from time to time in every country settled by the Normans – England, southern Italy, Palestine; but in Ireland it became almost the normal state of affairs. During the thirty years that followed John's death the great baronial families, the de Lacys, the Marshals, the Fitzgeralds, the de Burghs, struggled over land and succession. In the 'war of Meath' and the 'war of Kildare' they formed alliances and counter-alliances with one another and with Irish kings, while the justiciars, feebly supported from England, found it impossible to maintain order. In these wars the strength of the invaders was steadily drained away, and here may be found one of the root causes of the later decay of Norman power. But this weakness was not immediately apparent, and in spite of civil strife the area of Norman influence continued to expand. The de Burghs and their allies broke into Connaught; the Fitzgeralds (or 'Geraldines') established themselves in Munster and laid the basis of a power that was to survive until the sixteenth century; in Ormond the Butlers founded a dynasty that was to last even longer.

By the beginning of the fourteenth century, when this expansion had reached its limits, almost two-thirds of the island had been brought under the control of the Normans. Their power extended right round the eastern and southern coasts from Carrickfergus to Cape Clear. Inland it stretched in two broad bands, westwards to Connaught and south-westwards to Kerry. But the Irish, though territorially and politically divided, were still strong. In the north, Irish kings ruled over most of what is now the province of Ulster, scarcely disturbed by Norman power. In Connaught, the O'Connors retained a part of their ancient kingdom. In Thomond, O'Brien held his own against de Clare. In the more mountainous parts of Leinster and Munster, and in the wooded and boggy central plain, many Irish kings still maintained some degree of independent rule over part of their former dominions.

In spite of civil wars and racial divisions the government of the lordship became stronger in the latter half of the thirteenth century. Most of the settled area was divided up into counties, each with its own sheriff and with its shire-court where the itinerant justices administered the common law. As in England, some lands were governed as feudal liberties, in which the direct operation of royal authority was restricted. But the liberties no less than the counties were subject to the common law; and when it became customary to summon 'knights of the shire' to parliament the liberties also were called upon to send representatives. The parliament of 1297, for example, drew its members from nine counties: Connaught, Cork, Dublin, Kerry, Kildare, Limerick, Louth, Tipperary, Waterford; and five liberties: Carlow, Kilkenny, Meath, Ulster, Wexford. These lists give a fair idea of the territory to which the Anglo-Norman pattern of government had been applied at this time. Membership of the medieval Irish parliament was virtually confined to the settlers, its language was French and its legislation was effective only within the occupied area. But in law its authority extended over all Ireland. The independent or semi-independent Irish kings remained outside the system of counties and liberties, but their lands were part of the 'lordship' and it was the justiciar's duty to maintain contact with them. Very often, it is true, the government was at war with one or more of them; but the justiciar had authority to receive them back into the king's peace, and to protect them from damage so long as they remained within it. This authority over the Irish lands was purely external, exercised through the native ruler, and it was sometimes very shadowy, but it provided a link to hold together the Anglo-Norman and Irish elements in the country in some sort of constitutional relationship. In the early years of the fourteenth century the Anglo-Norman element appeared to be getting stronger. Edward I had compelled the magnates to remain at peace with one another, and the general success of his rule was shown by the extent to which he was able to draw men and supplies from Ireland for his Scottish wars. The more effectively the settled area was governed the more likely it was to expand; and at the end of Edward's reign there seemed, superficially at least, no reason why expansion should not continue until all Ireland had been shired, the intermediate authority of the Irish kings abolished, and the whole lordship brought directly under the rule of the common law.

The failure of this prospect has often been attributed to the Scottish invasion of Ireland in 1315. But though the invasion certainly gave a fatal blow to the authority of the central government, there were already serious weaknesses in the Norman position, which might, by themselves, have brought the lordship to virtual ruin. Above all, the number of settlers was too small. The first wave of conquest had been followed by a fairly steady stream of knights and barons, but there was no solid body of English or Anglo-Norman middle-class population. English and French merchants were established in some of the towns, notably in Dublin, and William Marshall settled small free-holders of English birth in parts of Leinster, but generally speaking, even in the areas most firmly held by the Normans, the bulk of the people were Irish. In the more remote areas of Connaught and Ulster the Norman veneer was very thin indeed. Almost inevitably, these isolated settlers began to adopt some of the habits, and even the language, of their neighbours; before the end of the thirteenth century the Irish parliament found it necessary to pass laws against 'degenerate' Englishmen, who 'attire themselves in Irish garments and having their heads half-shaven grow and extend the hairs from the back of the head . . . conforming themselves to the Irish as well in garb as in countenance'. (For the description of the colonists as 'English' see page 29.) But the process could not be arrested by statute, and as time went on many of the settlers conformed more and more to the Irish way of life. This basic weakness in the Norman position gave the Irish an opportunity for recovery. At no time during the middle ages was there anything like a united, much less a 'national', resistance to the conquest. But individual Irish rulers, though fighting for their own interests and though generally ready to recognize the overlordship of the king of England, did set limits to Norman expansion. After the middle of the thirteenth century their military inferiority was partly remedied by the importation of mercenary troops from the Hebrides. These 'gallowglasses' (*gall-óglaigh*: foreign soldiers) were of mixed Gaelic and Norse descent and their standard weapon was the great Scandinavian axe. Unlike the native Irish they wore body-armour, and they fought with a skill and determination that made them the backbone of every Irish army from the thirteenth century to the sixteenth. This Irish recovery had not achieved any decisive success before the Scottish invasion, but it was an important factor in the situation; for the continued resistance of the Irish, especially in the north, encouraged the Bruces to make the venture.

The hero of the invasion was Edward Bruce, brother of King Robert. In May 1315 he landed on the Antrim coast with 6000 Scottish troops and a year later he was crowned 'king of Ireland' at Dundalk. But the title meant little. Despite the high-sounding terms in which Donal O'Neill, 'king of Ulster and by hereditary right true heir to the whole of Ireland', professed to transfer his claims to Bruce, there was in fact no unity and no stability among the Irish. Some joined the Scots, more took advantage of the general disorder to engage in local war against their Norman enemies; but, though Bruce won victory after victory, there was no sign of that national resistance which in Scotland had finally established the unity and independence of the kingdom against the foreigner. At length, in October 1318, excommunicated by the pope, ill-supported or deserted by his Irish allies and with his own forces depleted, he was overthrown and killed at Faughart, not far from the scene of his coronation. It is significant that the native Irish annalists, in recording the events of these years, are chiefly impressed by the ferocity with which the war was conducted and the misery that it produced. To them Bruce is not the champion of Irish independence, but a usurper at whose death they rejoice: 'Edward Bruce, the destroyer of all Ireland in general, both foreigner and Gael, was slain by the foreigners of Ireland, through the power of battle and bravery, at Dundalk . . . and no better deed for the men of all Ireland was performed since the beginning of the world.'

The later middle ages

The fatal effects of the Scottish invasion upon the government of the lordship were not at once fully apparent. Bruce had failed to win the united support of the native Irish, he had not established a firm hold on any part of the country, and his death was followed by the complete abandonment of his enterprise. For a time it seemed as if the central government might recover the authority it had lost. Donal O'Neill was driven back to the interior of Ulster, other Irish rulers were forced to make peace and the few discontented Anglo-Norman nobles who had supported Bruce returned to their allegiance. But the shock to administration had been too great to admit of any permanent recovery. Disorder and plunder had drained the resources of the country, and bad harvests had added to the general distress. The whole basis of the settlement had been shaken, weaknesses were made more dangerous and disruptive forces given freer play.

The most immediate threat was that from the native Irish. Since the first arrival of the Normans the struggle between the races had been almost continuous, but throughout the thirteenth century the general result of the fighting had been the extension of the occupied area; and though by the beginning of the fourteenth the Norman advance was being generally held in check, yet even in the midst of the Bruce wars the Irish of Connaught suffered their heaviest defeat.

At Athenry, in 1316, the de Burghs and their allies destroyed a great Irish army and re-established their supremacy in the west; henceforth the O'Connor 'kingdom of Connaught' was reduced to a fraction of its former size and its ruler became little more than a dependant of the de Burghs. But this was the last important expansion of Norman power, and it proved a temporary one. Though the Irish would not unite, they were ready to take advantage of the disorder produced by the Scottish invasion to engage in local wars for the recovery of occupied lands. Their efforts were not consistently maintained nor universally successful, but they showed that the tide had turned. The thinness of the settlement and the practice of leaving enclaves of native territory in the settled areas now began to produce their effects.

While it suffered from these external attacks Norman power was also being weakened from within. The population of the settlement was declining. The towns suffered severely from the Black Death in 1349 and 1350, and there was a steady drift back to England, resulting from the poverty and insecurity of the country. This evil of 'absenteeism' had already drawn the anxious attention of the king, and in various forms plagued Ireland for centuries to come. It began with the greater barons, who had lands and interests in England or on the continent as well as in Ireland and who were often inclined to neglect their Irish responsibilities. Thus, garrisons were allowed to decay, and the sub-tenants were left to defend themselves as best they could against the Irish, or to come to terms with them. In such circumstances they were unlikely to have much respect for their nominal lords in England or for a government which did so little to protect them. The dangers of the situation were obvious, and as early as 1297 a law was enacted to compel absentees to make due provision for the protection of their lands. But no penalties were sufficient to enforce such legislation, and the frequency with which the government returned to the task is itself evidence of failure. As the Irish revival spread and strengthened, the pressure upon the remaining settlers increased; and now it was the whole body and not just the magnates who were affected. In 1361 Edward III complained of 'the magnates of our land of England', who, having estates in Ireland, 'take the profits thereof, but do not defend them'; in 1421 it was the 'artificers and labourers' who were so 'burdened with divers intolerable charges and wars' that they were flocking daily from Ireland to England. The development was ominous for the future of the settlement.

Amid these dangers, civil strife among the great Norman families tended to increase rather than to diminish. Its result was often to weaken the links which bound them to the crown and to leave their lands open to Irish reconquest. One example must suffice, but it amply illustrates the essential weakness of the lordship at this period. The powerful family of de Burgh had not only established its supremacy over Connaught but had also succeeded to the earldom of Ulster, where Richard (the 'Red Earl') had done something to remedy, for a time at least, the ill-effects of the Bruce invasion. But his grandson William (the 'Brown Earl') quarrelled bitterly with his own cousins and in 1333 he was murdered at Carrickfergus at their instigation. This might have mattered little had there been a son to succeed, but William's sole heiress was an infant daughter, who was carried off to England by her mother, and almost immediately the de Burgh inheritance began to break up. In the north, most of the lands that had once comprised the 'earldom of Ulster' fell to O'Neill and O'Doherty. In Connaught the development was different, but no less disastrous for royal authority. Here two brothers of the younger branch of the de Burghs defied the feudal law of succession and divided the family lands between them. Their surname had already been Gaelicized into 'Burke' and they now took the additional name 'MacWilliam', from their father William 'Liath' ('the Grey'). Speaking the Irish language, following Irish customs and inter-marrying with Irish families, they themselves virtually became Irish chieftains and lost almost all remnants of their feudal character. Elizabeth de Burgh, the legitimate heiress to Ulster and Connaught, was eventually married to Lionel, son of Edward III. His efforts to enforce his rights were fruitless; but through this marriage the claim passed into the English royal family, to be revived later on by the Tudors.

As the fourteenth century progressed it became more and more evident that there was little prospect of turning the lordship of Ireland into an effective feudal state embracing the whole country. Instead, the government was forced to concentrate on maintaining rather than on extending the settled area. This policy involved implicit recognition of the fact that the lordship was in reality a foreign colony in the midst of a hostile population, to be kept in existence only by constant border warfare. There was no formal abatement of the full claims of the English crown in Ireland, but in the later middle ages the contrast between those claims and the crown's actual authority, a contrast which had always existed, became much more strongly marked. It appears particularly in the shrinking of the area over which the Dublin government functioned regularly; before the end of the fourteenth century this 'English land' or 'land of peace' was confined to about one-third of the whole country, for by this time most of Ulster and Connaught and much of Munster had passed beyond effective control. But the contrast is also to be seen in a changed attitude to the native Irish. So long as there was a prospect of completing the conquest it was natural to look forward to the assimilation of the races and so to consider favourably the general extension of English law to the native population. Edward I, who was to have experience of the same kind of problem in Wales, had made an unsuccessful attempt to carry out such an extension in the 1270s. Even after the Bruce invasion, another effort was made by Edward III; but though many individuals and families were separately admitted to the privilege of English law it was now too late for a policy of general assimilation to succeed. The Irish were on the attack, the security of the settlement was threatened, and the almost inevitable result was a defensive 'colonial' policy, which finds its fullest expression in the famous 'statutes of Kilkenny'.

These statutes were passed in a parliament which met at Kilkenny in 1366 before Lionel, duke of Clarence, lieutenant in Ireland of his father King Edward III. They included measures for the better defence of the marches against the Irish enemy, for the prohibition of private warfare and for the regulation of trade. But by far the most important were those which aimed at setting a permanent barrier between the two races in Ireland, for it was recognized that wherever they mingled it was the Gaelic influence which predominated. So alliance between them by marriage or concubinage or by fostering of children was forbidden; neither the English (i.e. the Anglo-Norman settlers) nor 'the Irish living amongst the English' were to use the Irish language; the English were not to use Irish names, Irish dress, Irish law, nor to ride without saddles after the fashion of the Irish, Existing laws which excluded Irishmen from cathedral chapters, ecclesiastical benefices and religious houses amongst the English were re-enacted. The statutes of Kilkenny have often been represented as a kind of aggressive 'outlawing' of the Irish; in fact, they were essentially defensive, directed towards preserving royal authority and English influence in what still remained intact of the lordship. To give them greater force, the three archbishops and five bishops present at the parliament published sentence of excommunication against all who should contravene them.

The Kilkenny policy, though supported by these spiritual sanctions and fortified by later enactments, could not be fully carried out. In the church, it is true, the segregation of English and Irish clergy, which was of long standing, was fairly consistently maintained. The distinction was heightened by the fact that in areas where the native clergy were still in control the reforms of the twelfth century had in some respects left little permanent mark on the life of the church. There was no strictly parochial system; bishoprics and religious houses continued to be associated with particular families; even the practice of hereditary succession in ecclesiastical benefices had not disappeared. The dioceses which were 'among the English' were certainly not free from abuses, but in general they stood for a more orderly system of administration. This contrast strengthened the alliance between crown and papacy, and together they managed to exclude the native Irish from the most important posts in the 'English' area. The bishops, abbots and other clergy who attended parliaments or councils were almost without exception of English birth or descent, and their attitude towards their Irish fellow-churchmen seems to have been dictated entirely by considerations of political interest and racial antipathy.

But the segregation which had been established and maintained in the church was impossible in secular life, and the mingling of the races could not be prevented. In Connaught and in the earldom of Ulster the process had already gone too far for any change to be attempted. The 'degenerate English', as they came to be called, were not likely to change their long-established habits at the bidding of parliament. Even in Munster and Leinster, where royal authority was still of some force, the Geraldines and Butlers and other leading families were too well aware of the benefits they derived from their intimate contacts with the Irish to give them up. Throughout the later fourteenth century and the whole of the fifteenth, as the real authority of the Dublin government receded, Irish language, Irish law and Irish dress became more and more prevalent, even in the districts which had once been most thoroughly settled. In the more remote areas the settlers became, as the old saying has it, 'more Irish than the Irish themselves'.

It must not be supposed that in this mingling of races the influence was all on one side and that the Irish remained completely unaffected. Irish rulers copied the Anglo-Normans in various ways. They adopted crests and coats of arms, they used seals, issued charters, entered into indentures and made written treaties. These changes, though not unimportant in themselves, were only symbols of something much deeper, which touched the core of the Gaelic political system. The main weakness of that system was the absence of direct hereditary succession by primogeniture; instead, when a ruler died a successor was elected from among the members of his family. An attempt to secure continuity was often made by electing a 'tanist', or prospective successor, in the lifetime of a reigning king or chief, but this was a clumsy and sometimes a dangerous procedure. Besides, natural dynastic ambition made many an Irish ruler anxious to establish a family power by direct succession, and the superior advantages of a political system based on the hereditary holding of land were very attractive. These factors working together led to a partial feudalization of the Gaelic political system, which appeared particularly in the increased personal power of the chiefs, supported by the employment of gallowglasses under the chief's personal command. These developments did not take place without protest and resistance. In particular, all attempts to establish hereditary succession by primogeniture as a fixed rule were unavailing; but they were not abandoned, and dynastic ambitions and rivalries go far to account for the succession-wars which tore almost every part of the country in the fifteenth century, and for the readiness with which Irish rulers accepted feudal grants of their lands from Henry VIII in the sixteenth.

The decline of royal authority after the Bruce wars had shown itself not only in a growing inability to resist Irish attacks, but also in the weakening of the links which bound the settlers to England. In one sense these links had never been strong. The statutes of Kilkenny are prefaced by a declaration that 'at the conquest of the land of Ireland and for a long time after, the English of the said land used the English language'. But in reality, the twelfth-century conquerors were Normans and spoke French, the language, indeed, in which the statutes of Kilkenny are themselves written. Just as the Normans in England gradually abandoned the use of French and took to English, the Normans in Ireland, or a considerable proportion of them, as naturally took to Irish. In the trading towns, of course, and in the districts around them, and among the more important families, whose contacts with England were fairly close, English came to be spoken. But even before the end of the thirteenth century, and without any suggestion of a linguistic test, we find the settlers in general referred to as 'Englishmen'. They were, however, English with a difference, and the distinction between 'English born in

Ireland' and 'English born in England' remained a constantly recurring theme at least down to the eighteenth century. The statutes of Kilkenny tried to obliterate the distinction, but in vain, for it represented a real diversity of outlook and interest.

The 'English born in Ireland' (or, as we may now begin to call them, the Anglo-Irish*), though they might profess formal loyalty to the crown, were not always ready to support its authority. From the beginning of the conquest the magnates had aimed at building up family supremacies, usually fortified by alliances with Irish chiefs – a policy which the statutes of Kilkenny had been unable to check. They did not, of course, ignore the machinery of royal government, but when opportunity offered they were always ready to control it in their own interests rather than in those of the crown. Thus the crown was almost compelled to rely for the maintenance of its authority upon Englishmen born, and the policy of appointing them to the most important posts in the Irish administration was followed fairly consistently from the foundation of the lordship. English kings were not prepared to visit Ireland regularly, nor to devote to a military conquest of the country supplies of men and money comparable to those which they poured out on their Welsh, Scottish and French wars, but they were at least anxious that within the area controlled by the Dublin government the royal authority should be respected. Thus, the Irish law courts were subordinate to the English; English legislation was applied to Ireland, sometimes with the additional sanction of the Irish parliament but sometimes also without it; the Irish treasurer was called on to account to the English exchequer, and other officials of the Irish government might be obliged to defend themselves in English courts. Down to the latter part of the fifteenth century these means were sufficient to prevent the domination of the Dublin administration by an Anglo-Irish magnate.

But though the crown could keep fairly consistent control of the government of the lordship, it could not prevent that government from becoming steadily weaker. On all sides the Irish were pushing once more into the territory they had lost. In the north Niall More O'Neill had made himself virtually king of Ulster, destroying all but a few remnants of the Norman earldom; he even extended his authority into Connaught, where royal authority was now little more than

*The term 'Anglo-Irish' is used here for convenience; but, though it occurs occasionally from the medieval period onwards, it did not gain general currency until the nineteenth century, when it was most commonly applied to the descendants of the seventeenth-century English settlers.

a name. In Munster the O'Kennedys, once the subordinate allies of the earls of Ormond, seized and held territories which the Butlers could no longer defend; and both in Munster and in Meath other Irish clans were making similar conquests. The Irish revival in Leinster was even more dangerous. In the mountainous region to the south of Dublin Art MacMurrough Kavanagh, claimant to the old Irish kingdom of Leinster, was steadily enlarging his territories and stretching out into the fertile lowlands to east and west, thus building up a strong Gaelic state within striking distance of the capital. But this Irish expansion reflected the personal ambition of the chiefs rather than any 'national' movement. Richard II received personal homage from both Niall More O'Neill and Art MacMurrough when visiting Ireland in 1394, and the latter was knighted by the king's hand. It is significant also that Art MacMurrough sought the alliance of the earl of Kildare and strengthened it by marrying the earl's sister, despite the statutes of Kilkenny.

The weakening of Anglo-Irish loyalty and the growth of native power combined to restrict the authority of the Dublin government more and more to a narrow strip of territory on the east coast. Richard II, during his visit to Ireland in 1394–5, proposed to recognize this fact, to strengthen a definitely 'English land' between Dundalk and Waterford and use it as a base from which royal authority might be re-established over at least part of the rest of the country. Richard himself had not the resources to put this policy into execution and his Lancastrian successors were too busily employed in foreign and domestic wars to attempt it. By the middle of the fifteenth century the 'English land', or 'English Pale', as it came to be called, had shrunk to much narrower limits than those which Richard had planned; and so far from being a base for the recovery of the rest of the country it lived almost in a state of siege, obliged sometimes to buy off the Irish on its borders by the payment of 'black rents'. It would, however, be misleading to suppose that beyond the Pale the force of royal authority had completely disappeared; over a fairly wide area it was still formally recognized and sometimes actually asserted. Eleven counties, of which Limerick was the most remote, contributed to the parliamentary subsidies of 1421; parliamentary writs continued to be sent to the sheriffs of Ulster and Connaught; parliament itself occasionally met in towns far outside the Pale – in Wexford in 1463, in Limerick twenty years later. Thus, even at its lowest ebb, the Dublin government never abandoned the claim to the lordship of Ireland. More than this, it maintained a

Later Medieval Ireland

Showing area of the Pale and distribution of some of
the most important Irish and Anglo-Irish families

bridgehead. The ports of Dublin, Drogheda, Dundalk and Waterford were open to English shipping and offered ready inlets to any English king who was prepared to send forces to reassert his power in Ireland. The way was open, both legally and physically, for re-conquest; but the significance of this did not become clear until the sixteenth century.

During most of the fifteenth century, while England was being drained by the disastrous campaigns in France and torn by civil strife, Ireland was left to go pretty much its own way. The Anglo-Irish were to some extent affected by the wars of the Roses, which for them, however, proved little more than a new phase of an old struggle between Geraldines and Butlers. The former, supported by most of the Anglo-Irish nobles, were Yorkists, the latter Lancastrians. The popularity of the Yorkist cause arose at least in part from the great reputation achieved by Richard of York as lord lieutenant between 1447 and 1460. He had no genuine interest in Ireland, but there were both Irish and Anglo-Irish strains in his ancestry; and more than this, in an effort to manipulate the politics of the Pale to the advantage of his own party, he supported a claim to legislative and judicial independence put forward in the Irish parliament. Despite this alliance, the Yorkist triumph with the accession of Edward IV in 1461 made no important change in Anglo-Irish relationships. The really significant development of the next two decades was the rise of the Leinster Geraldines under the earls of Kildare. The way to power lay open, for after Thomas, seventh earl of Desmond, had been attainted and executed at Drogheda in 1468 the Munster Geraldines withdrew from the politics of the Pale, and the influence of the pro-Lancastrian Butlers was in decline under a Yorkist monarchy.

The Kildare influence had been steadily increasing for over a century, but it was not until the 1470s that it became dominant. The seventh earl was deputy* at the time of his death in 1477. The council, which was controlled by the Kildare party, immediately elected his son, Gerald (or Garret), the 'Great Earl' ('Garret More' to the Irish), as justiciar to carry on the government until the king should make a new appointment. Edward IV attempted to curtail this rising power by sending over an English deputy, Lord Grey,

---

*The deputy took the place of the lord lieutenant, at this period usually an absentee, to whom the government of Ireland was nominally entrusted; but the deputy was directly responsible to the king.

A.S.H.O.I.–B

instead of confirming Kildare in office, as the Anglo-Irish had expected. But Edward's attempt failed. Kildare refused to recognize Grey, the chancellor refused to hand over the great seal, the constable of Dublin Castle refused to surrender his command, and in the end the king had to give in. Kildare paid a visit to England and he accepted various conditions, but he came back as deputy, and the family power of the Kildares, thus established even against the king himself, dominated Irish politics for two generations.

The source of this family power was threefold. In the first place it arose from Kildare's position as a territorial magnate, whose earldom, stretching over the modern counties of Kildare and Carlow and lying partly inside and partly outside the Pale, enabled him to exercise an almost irresistible influence on the Dublin government. Secondly, the Great Earl extended the policy of building up alliances among the native Irish, fortified by political marriages. It was the power derived from these two sources that enabled him to make effective use of the third, his control of the deputyship. By itself, this conferred little independent authority, but Kildare was strong enough to use it for his own ends. Council and parliament gave legal sanction to his actions; the military resources of the Pale became virtually part of his private army; the royal revenue was almost as freely at his disposal as the revenue of his own estates.

The accession of the Tudors to the English throne made little immediate difference in Ireland. Henry VII followed, of necessity, a waiting and defensive policy; and Kildare, despite his known adherence to the Yorkist cause, was allowed to remain deputy. Even after he had openly challenged Henry's authority by crowning Lambert Simnel as 'Edward VI' in Christ Church cathedral, Dublin, he was continued in office. A few years later, however, the more serious threat from the intrigues surrounding Perkin Warbeck forced Henry into action; and for a brief period he tried the experiment of ruling Ireland through an English deputy, backed by an English army. The deputy was Sir Edward Poynings, a capable soldier, who succeeded in foiling Warbeck's attempted invasion in 1495. But the expense of this system of government was heavy and it soon became clear that the Irish revenue could not be increased sufficiently to meet it. Besides this, the most urgent danger from Warbeck quickly shifted to the Anglo-Scottish border, where James IV was preparing to assist him by force of arms. So Poynings and the English troops were recalled, and after a brief interval Kildare was restored.

Poynings' administration left one enduring memorial in the famous statute which bears his name. 'Poynings' law', which remained in force, with various modifications, until the legislative union of 1800, was enacted in a parliament at Drogheda in 1494. In its original form it laid down that no parliament was to meet in Ireland until the chief governor and council had first informed the king and council in England of the reasons why a parliament was necessary and of the bills to be proposed to it, and had received licence under the great seal of England to proceed. In later years this law came to be the great clog on the initiative of the Irish parliament. But fifteenth-century parliaments, English or Irish, rarely took the initiative in legislation, and the law was intended to curb over-powerful deputies; by the peaceful citizens of the Pale it was looked upon as a protective and not an oppressive measure.

The restoration of Kildare in 1496 was a clear indication that Henry's policy in Ireland was strictly defensive. He wanted to secure the quiet government of the country as cheaply as possible, and in this he succeeded. Warbeck's last attempt at invasion was driven off in 1497; and for over twenty years, in spite of the increasing naval power and national rivalries of the European states, none of them attempted to weaken the English king by intrigues with his Anglo-Irish subjects. The Great Earl ruled continuously until his death in 1513, extending his influence, through his estates and his alliances, over the greater part of the country and defeating every combination of his enemies, but maintaining at the same time an unshaken loyalty to the English crown. When he died his son 'Garret Oge' (Young Gerald) succeeded almost as naturally to the deputyship as to the earldom. But this peaceful succession marked the beginning of a new and dangerous era, for English policy towards Ireland was changing in a way which would soon leave no room for the feudal independence of the house of Kildare.

2 The Tudor conquest

The fall of the house of Kildare

The succession of the ninth earl of Kildare almost coincided with
the advent of Wolsey to power in England; and it may have been
under Wolsey's guidance that Henry VIII began to show a more
active concern about Irish affairs. Certainly the state of the country
did not conform to Tudor ideas of royal authority. The government
of the Pale, though carried on in the king's name, was really in the
hands of Kildare and his Anglo-Irish dependants. The Pale itself was
still confined within its old narrow frontiers, and even Kildare could
not always defend it against incursions by hostile Irish. Beyond the
Pale Ireland presented a political patchwork which an English writer
of the period has described as follows:

There be more than sixty countries, called regions, in Ireland, inhabited
with the king's Irish enemies . . . where reigneth more than sixty captains . . . that liveth by the sword and obeyeth to no other temporal
person, but only to himself that is strong: and every of the said captains
maketh war and peace for himself, and holdeth by the sword, and hath
imperial jurisdiction within his room, and obeyeth to no other person,
English or Irish, except only to such persons as may subdue him by the
sword. . . . Also, there is more than thirty great captains of the English
noble folk, that followeth the same Irish order . . . and every of them
maketh war and peace for himself, without any licence of the king, or of
any other temporal person, save of him that is strongest, and of such as
may subdue them by the sword.

The boundaries of these 'regions' or petty states (*tuatha* in Irish)
were constantly fluctuating; there were conflicting claims to supremacy in this or that area; alliances and counter-alliances were
constantly in course of formation or disintegration; and local warfare, which sometimes spread until it embraced almost the whole
island, was endemic.

Powerful as the Great Earl had been, it was beyond his strength,
perhaps beyond his desire, to impose order on this chaos. He had

been satisfied to retain the deputyship and use its prestige and authority to strengthen his own family. His son was to discover that this policy could not long survive active royal intervention from England.

Henry's concern about Ireland did not extend, at least to begin with, to territories under Gaelic rule. His primary purpose was to strengthen direct royal authority over the government in Dublin and to bring the Anglo-Norman lordships beyond the boundaries of the Pale more effectively under royal control. This new policy took time to develop and was not consistently pursued. Though Kildare was summoned to London in 1515 to give an account of his government, he was allowed to return to Ireland as deputy with undiminished powers. In 1519, however, he was summoned again; and this time there was a strict inquiry into his conduct, with the result that he was removed from office; and now the principles of a new system of Irish government were clearly laid down. Private war was to be suppressed; Wolsey's legatine authority was to be enforced and the ecclesiastical administration reformed; a parliament was to be summoned and a subsidy collected from all Ireland. The man chosen to carry out this policy was Thomas Howard, earl of Surrey, who was to hold rank not as lord deputy but as lord lieutenant, the first resident lieutenant since the mid fifteenth century. Surrey was a capable soldier, a great nobleman and lord admiral of England; thus he might hope to out-shine Kildare and attract the respect and loyalty which had been refused to a civil servant like Poynings.

The experiment was not a success. Surrey reached Dublin in May 1520 and immediately found himself in difficulties. The Irish ex-chequer was nearly empty, and the £4000 which he had brought with him was soon exhausted. Almost immediately after his arrival O'Neill invaded the Pale from the north, and though a brief campaign produced temporary peace the situation remained precarious. In the late summer plague broke out in the Pale, and food prices shot up to famine level. By November Surrey was almost at his wit's end – 'I and the treasurer with all the captains of the king's retinues here have not amongst us all £20 in money.' Some relief from England and some increase in the Irish revenue enabled him to carry on for a time. But Henry warned him not to expect continued heavy payments out of the English treasury and urged him to reduce Ireland by diplomacy, to proceed 'by sober ways, politic drifts and amiable persuasions'. Surrey was in a better position than his master to judge the realities of the situation. At the end of his first year he sent the king a report arguing that Ireland could be reduced only by force and pointing out the implications of such a policy in men and money. When Henry refused to face these implications Surrey asked to be recalled: 'I have continued here one year and a half, to your grace's great charges and to mine undoing, for I have spent all that I might make.' A few months later he was allowed to lay down his office.

Surrey's viceroyalty had revealed how expensive direct government of this kind could be: between April 1520 and March 1522 more than £18,000 of English money had been sent over to Ireland; and there was no early prospect that the Irish revenue could be increased to anything like this extent. In these circumstances, Henry reverted, for a time, to the old policy of governing through an Anglo-Irish noble; but he took precautions against any revival of the 'all but kingship' formerly exercised by the Kildares, partly by strengthening the authority of the council in Dublin but mainly by fairly frequent changes in the deputyship. In March 1522, after Surrey's removal, Sir Piers Butler, earl of Ormond, who was Kildare's chief Anglo-Irish rival, was made deputy. In 1524, he was removed and Kildare was reappointed. In 1526 both men were summoned to England; and Kildare, though he retained the title of deputy, was kept there under restraint. Butler was obliged to surrender the earldom of Ormond to a rival claimant (Sir Thomas Boleyn), but was compensated with that of Ossory and was allowed to return to Ireland. In 1528 Kildare was dismissed and Butler became deputy once again.

These frequent changes show that Irish affairs were now of more continuous concern to the king and his advisers than they had been during the previous reign; but there is little to suggest that any long-term policy was emerging. The end to be aimed at was recognized clearly enough; but Henry was unwilling to face the expense that would necessarily be incurred in attaining it. He did, however, make a brief and half-hearted return to the policy of ruling Ireland through an English governor; and in 1530 he sent over Sir William Skeffington, a professional soldier who had recent experience of Irish warfare, with a small body of English troops. But Skeffington was not given adequate support, either political or military. Kildare, who had been allowed to return to Ireland, was determined to thwart 'the gunner', as he called him in derision; and through his friends on the Irish council and at the English court he succeeded in undermining Skeffington's position and bringing about his recall in the summer of 1532. In his place, Kildare himself was appointed deputy, probably because Henry had now come to the conclusion that if Ireland was to be governed by an Anglo-Irish noble, only Kildare had the prestige and the resources necessary to do so effectively without financial or military support from England.

At first sight it might appear that things had now returned to the position in which they stood at the opening of the reign. But, in fact, the events of the intervening years had brought about a radical change. The long continuity of Kildare rule had been broken; and the ninth earl could not, at this stage, recover the dominant position he had inherited from his father. Besides this, the government in London now kept a watchful eye on Irish affairs; and Thomas Cromwell, who had succeeded Wolsey as Henry's chief adviser, readily listened to the complaints that Kildare's enemies, and especially the Butlers, sent over. As a result, Kildare was summoned to England. It is likely that a decision to remove him from office had already been taken; but when he left Ireland in February 1534 he was still deputy and was allowed to leave his son, Lord Offaly ('Silken Thomas'), as lord justice in his place.

In retrospect, the year 1534 can be seen as a turning point in Irish history; and from this time onwards we can trace a gradual extension of direct royal authority over the whole country. The process was maintained with varying degrees of intensity and by methods of diplomacy as well as of war, and it was defensive rather than aggressive in purpose; but it led to a complete military conquest at the end of Elizabeth's reign. Probably some such development was inevitable: the Tudor monarchy could not for ever tolerate the existence on its western flank of a half-subdued dependency which, if not controlled by England, might serve as a base for England's continental enemies. But there is nothing to indicate that Henry had any new forward policy in mind when he summoned Kildare to England; his hand was forced by the sudden insurrection of Kildare's son, who burst in upon the council chamber in Dublin, flung down the sword of office, and disowned his allegiance to the king. He was moved to this action by reports, assiduously spread by the enemies of his family, that his father had been put to death and that he himself would be the next victim. Though these reports had no basis in fact, there could be no doubt that the Kildare power was under threat; and it was natural that Thomas, a proud and fiery young man, should choose the path of violent resistance rather than submit. In face of this defiance, Henry had no option but to take effective military action; and from this the slow, intermittent and costly process of a systematic conquest gradually developed.

The struggle with the Kildare power went on intermittently for the next six years. Though government forces were small when the rebellion began, Thomas was in an awkward position. The citizens of Dublin were hostile, for their interest lay in firm rule and the maintenance of cross-channel trade, and in face of their hostility he could not capture the castle. The Butlers were loyal to the crown and on more than one occasion he was obliged to divert forces to defend his lands against them. The arrival of Sir William Skeffington with a strong English force soon deprived him of effective control over any part of the Pale and compelled him to rely more than ever on his allies among the native Irish. The speedy fall of his principal stronghold, May-nooth castle, before Skeffington's artillery, was a warning that rebels could no longer rely upon immunity behind their fortifications, and the execution of most of the garrison showed that the day of easy pardons had gone. For a time Thomas's allies fell away, and he himself was captured and sent to England. But after a brief uneasy peace war broke out again more widely than ever, with Irish and Anglo-Irish throughout the whole country allied in a great 'Geraldine league'. This looked an imposing combination, but there were too many old jealousies and selfish ambitions for unity to last, and the league soon crumbled under the military defeats inflicted upon it by Skeffington's successor, Lord Leonard Grey. By 1540 the struggle was over. Not only was the power of the Leinster Geraldines broken, but the family was almost exterminated. The ninth earl had died in in prison, 'Silken Thomas' and five of his uncles had been executed at Tyburn, and the claimant to the earldom was a twelve-year-old boy in exile in France.

Henry VIII's new Irish policy

In 1540 Ireland lay open to conquest. With the disappearance of the Leinster Geraldines there was, for the time being, no force capable of resisting the crown. But Henry was not in a position to use the opportunity. His policy of ecclesiastical nationalism had raised dangers both at home and abroad and he was unwilling to commit himself too deeply in Ireland. Already the cost of maintaining government there was considerable. Even at the end of the reign, when royal authority seemed firmly established and the country was comparatively peaceful, Ireland was not self-supporting, but required an annual £5000 from the English treasury. There was nothing to spare for large-scale military undertakings.

Once more, therefore, Henry resolved to get what he could by diplomatic means, to revert to the 'sober ways, politic drifts and amiable persuasions' that he had recommended to Surrey twenty years earlier. Some beginning had been made already. In the first interval of the Kildare war a parliament had been summoned which had obediently enacted for Ireland the most important of the statutes passed by the 'reformation parliament' in England. The dissolution of religious houses had also begun and, as in England, liberal grants of monastic lands helped to reconcile the magnates (both Anglo-Irish and Irish) to the ecclesiastical changes. It was, perhaps, the ease with which parliament had been induced to accept Henry's wishes in 1537 that encouraged him to trust to peaceful methods in exploiting the final victory over the Leinster Geraldines.

The essence of Henry's policy was that the entire ruling class of Ireland should be brought into real dependence upon himself. So far as the Anglo-Irish were concerned this meant no more than the application of existing law. But the relationship between the native rulers and the lord of Ireland had always been ill-defined, and some radical change in their position was necessary if they were to form a loyal and active element in the state.

The execution of this policy was entrusted to Sir Anthony St Leger, appointed deputy in 1540 in succession to Lord Leonard Grey. He was well fitted for the task, for he was a soldier, a diplomat and an administrator, and he had already spent several years in Ireland. As a special commissioner from the king he had travelled over much of the country, both inside and outside the Pale, and he had been concerned in the management of parliament.

St Leger set to work by concluding a series of individual agreements with the more important Irish chiefs. Such agreements had long formed part of the regular pattern of Irish politics; but now they were concluded much more widely, and they contained provisions which established a new relationship between the chiefs and the crown. The agreement with Turlough O'Toole in November 1540 was a model for those that followed: he was to surrender his lands to Henry, to receive them back to be held by knight-service, to keep no private forces except with the consent of the deputy, and to use English laws and customs. These conditions formed the essence of the policy of 'surrender and re-grant' which, within the next few years, was applied to almost all Ireland and brought every Irish ruler into formal relationship with the crown. The more powerful of them were given English titles. Conn O'Neill became earl of Tyrone,

Murrough O'Brien became earl of Thomond, MacGilpatrick became baron of Upper Ossory, Donough O'Brien became baron of Ibrackin. 'Degenerate English' and rebellious Anglo-Irish returned to their allegiance and received similar treatment. MacWilliam Burke surrendered his lands and received them back with the title of earl of Clanricard; Desmond made public submission to the deputy and received the royal pardon.

The public declaration of the new policy came in June 1541, when a parliament specially summoned for the purpose conferred upon Henry the title 'king of Ireland'. The parliament was unusually well attended, and in addition to the Anglo-Irish ecclesiastics, nobles, gentry and citizens, so many Irish chiefs or their representatives were present that it was thought necessary to have the bill read over to them in their native language, and they too expressed their 'liberal consents'. The whole proceeding was carried through with great enthusiasm, and on the following Sunday the new title was publicly proclaimed in St Patrick's cathedral after a solemn mass sung by the archbishop of Dublin. Thus Henry made it clear that his right to Ireland did not depend upon papal grant, a ground upon which he could not now logically stand. The mere change of title meant little. But the dutiful presence of so many Anglo-Irish nobles and the representatives of so many counties, cities and boroughs, outside as well as inside the Pale, and, above all, the attendance of so many of the native Irish chiefs, were significant. It seemed as if the effective authority of the crown over the whole country was at last to be established, not by military conquest but by peaceful agreement.

In this policy Henry showed a more enlightened statesmanship than many of the Englishmen who have had to govern Ireland. His main objects were conciliation and fusion: the conciliation of the great by confirming them in their lands, granting them new titles and sharing with them the spoil of the religious houses; the fusion of the colonial and the native populations by a complete abandonment of the policy of segregation and by the extension of English law to the whole country. For a time Henry seemed to have succeeded. There was general submission to his claims. Anglo-Irish and Irish alike formally recognized him as king of Ireland and renounced 'the usurped authority of the bishop of Rome'. Thus the declaration of the kingdom of Ireland and the royal supremacy over the church were publicly endorsed by the leaders of the ruling class, native and colonial.

Whatever its merits and however great its temporary success, this policy failed. The cause is probably to be found, not in any single factor, but in the cumulative effect of many. The system of 'surrender and re-grant' ignored the Irish law of land tenure, by which the chief's right in the lands over which he ruled was not personal and hereditary but official and for life. Conn O'Neill and other ambitious chiefs were quite ready to accept these royal grants and to base upon them claims which they pushed to the utmost, in defiance of Irish law, against their allies and dependants. Thus the rank and file of the Irish gentry found themselves threatened with deprivation by their own leaders in alliance with the English king. St Leger had hoped that the new policy, by establishing the system of primogeniture, would end the chronic evil of internecine strife, but instead the evil was aggravated. Within a few years the legal heir to the earldom of Clanricard found himself opposed by a chief elected in the traditional fashion, and a similar dispute in the earldom of Tyrone helped to keep Ulster in a state of civil war for many years.

It is fairly easy to see how this clash of legal systems was likely to affect the success of Henry's policy. There are two other factors whose weight is harder to estimate. The ecclesiastical changes which accompanied the policy have sometimes been regarded as contributory to its failure; but this is only true in so far as these changes prepared the way for the protestantism of Edward VI's reign. The other doubtful factor is the nature of the Irish social system which Henry was trying to recast on peaceful English lines. Irish life was organized for war, not for peace. The Irish chief or Anglo-Irish lord was essentially a war-leader and in every Irish state the most influential class had a vested interest in fighting. In these circumstances it is hard to see how the royal peace could have been permanently imposed on the whole kingdom without a preliminary conquest. This is perhaps the fundamental reason for the failure of Henry's policy. In a sense, it might be regarded as a condemnation of his attempt to proceed by peaceful means; but he can hardly be blamed for not recognizing at the time what can be seen clearly only in retrospect.

The reformation

Though Henry VIII's ecclesiastical policy had been accepted in Ireland as readily as in England, the circumstances of the two countries were quite different. The Irish church was not strong enough or rich enough to excite the same degree of jealousy and greed among the secular nobles as was common elsewhere. It was split by the discord between 'Irish' and 'English' clergy; and frequent warfare made the regular collection of ecclesiastical dues very difficult. In some parts of the country the parish churches and even the cathedrals were ruinous; and benefices were often vacant or held by absentees, so that the people had to depend for spiritual ministrations upon the 'poor friars beggars'; and, at a later stage, the popular influence that the friars thus gained was to be of considerable importance. But the spirit of intellectual inquiry and criticism, the profound concern about questions of faith and order, which had been steadily growing for more than a century in other parts of Western Christendom, had hardly been felt in Ireland. The fact that the country had no university was itself an indication of its remoteness from the mainstream of European thought.

Though Ireland was thus unprepared for the protestant reformation, it was not likely to offer serious resistance to Henry's policy of 'catholicism without the pope'. The native Irish rulers had no reason for supporting papal authority, which had generally been exerted on the side of the English; the Anglo-Irish might naturally be expected to fall in line with a policy which had already been accepted in England. And this is in fact what happened. There was, to begin with, some opposition among the Anglo-Irish clergy, led by Archbishop Cromer of Armagh, and in the parliament of 1536–7 the clerical proctors raised some objections, which led to the final exclusion of the lower clergy from the Irish parliament. But when once the act of supremacy had been passed, the majority of the bishops seem to have conformed and the secular magnates made no bones about renouncing papal authority. It is true that the Geraldine party, both before and after the passing of the act of supremacy, used religion as a rallying cry. But this was due to the hope of securing foreign help at least as much as to conviction, and in the end none of the rebels hesitated to accept the royal supremacy as a condition of pardon. The apathy of the native Irish at this stage is shown in the failure of the Jesuit missionaries who arrived in Ulster in 1542 with letters from the pope and from Ignatius Loyola. The northern chiefs gave them such a scant welcome that they were soon glad to make their escape to Scotland. It is unlikely that the attitude of the bishops and secular magnates was widely shared by the common people, who were influenced against the royal supremacy by the teaching of the friars; but the danger of a popular opposition had not yet appeared; and for the time being Henry seemed to have succeeded.

So far, the course of the ecclesiastical revolution in Ireland had been almost exactly parallel with that in England. But with the attempt to use the royal supremacy to bring about changes in doctrine and liturgy the difference between the two countries at once appeared. Not only was there no strong reform party in Ireland to counter the inevitable opposition, but the changes came at a time when the country was entering upon a new period of political unrest. The weaknesses in Henry VIII's system of government have already been pointed out, and in the decade following his death these were aggravated by frequent changes in English policy and by the outbreak of war with France and the consequent activity of French envoys in Ireland. The superficial peace established by the policy of 'surrender and re-grant' disappeared in a series of Irish insurrections; and the defence of the Pale again became one of the deputy's main preoccupations.

It was in these most unfavourable circumstances that the government of Edward VI set about extending to Ireland the ecclesiastical changes that had already taken place in England. No Irish parliament was summoned and there was no formal synod or convocation of the clergy; but an edition of the English Book of Common Prayer of 1549 was printed in Dublin (the first book to be printed in Ireland) and its use enjoined by virtue of the royal prerogative. Except in the Pale and in a few cities and towns beyond it the government's policy had little effect. Over the greater part of the country church services went on as before. Even within the Pale the change was by no means universally acquiesced in; everywhere, among both Irish and Anglo-Irish, there was a strong spirit of opposition, and the few enthusiastic reformers among the bishops found little support. Many of the bishops and temporal rulers who had accepted the royal supremacy under Henry VIII were now ready, as in England, to return to papal authority as a necessary defence against doctrinal innovation. Such was George Dowdall, Henry's archbishop of Armagh and a strong supporter of royal supremacy in the church. He went into exile rather than accept the Book of Common Prayer, for 'he would never be a bishop where the holy mass was abolished'. Within a short time he had been reconciled with the papacy and was reappointed to his see by papal provision.

The reversal of policy which followed hard upon the death of Edward VI was almost universally welcomed in Ireland. As in England, the reforming bishops were deprived. But no proceedings were taken against them for heresy, and the fires of Smithfield and

Oxford, which lit the way for a protestant settlement in England, had no counterpart in Ireland. No doubt this arose mainly from the fact that there were so few protestants that there was no need to burn them; but it reflects also the difficulties of a government which had other and more urgent problems to attend to. Neither the attempted introduction of protestantism nor its abandonment had produced any fundamental change in the political situation, and in civil affairs Mary simply continued the policy of Edward VI. The formal restoration of papal authority did nothing to reconcile the native Irish to English rule and her reign was almost wholly occupied in military operations against them.

When Elizabeth succeeded to the throne it was inevitable that she should extend to Ireland the protestant policy that circumstances had compelled her to adopt in England. But this did not involve any radical change in the central administration; indeed, Elizabeth appointed as deputy the earl of Sussex, who had held the same post under Mary, and who was now to preside over the reversal of the ecclesiastical policy of Mary's reign. As in England, the new church settlement was a parliamentary one, and it was based mainly upon acts of supremacy and uniformity almost identical with those passed in England. The parliament which passed them met in Dublin in January 1560 and was dissolved barely three weeks later. The speed with which such controversial measures were got through, in spite of very strong opposition, has been used as an argument in favour of the theory that they were either passed by a trick or not passed at all but simply added to the statute book. The truth probably is that the members, elected under government supervision, carried out, however reluctantly, government policy. The number of bishops present at the parliament is uncertain; but the bishops in general made no public opposition to the acts and only two of them openly refused to take the oath of supremacy. Nevertheless, the act of uniformity was not – indeed could not be – generally enforced, and acceptance of the royal supremacy did not necessarily mean acceptance of the Book of Common Prayer.

The legislation of 1560 marks the formal close of the Irish reformation. But in another sense it is only a beginning, for the reformed church had as yet few adherents in any part of the country. Even in the Pale Elizabeth dared not risk alienating the loyal Anglo-Irish by a rigid enforcement of the act of uniformity, and throughout a great part of the country the government had not the means of doing so even if it had desired. If little could be done by force not much was accomplished by persuasion. The bishops and clergy in general showed no missionary zeal, and various projects for publishing the Bible and prayer book in Irish were postponed until it was too late. For the field of enterprise thus neglected by the reformed clergy was soon seized upon by the Jesuits and missionary priests from the continent whose labours, supplementing those of the friars, laid the foundation of that devotion to the Roman Catholic faith which has long been characteristic of the bulk of the population of Ireland.

In Elizabeth's reign, also, the political consequences of the reformation began to appear. The papacy, for so long the ally of English power in Ireland, now became its enemy, and a religious bitterness was added to the old struggle. This change complicated the position of the Anglo-Irish – the 'Old English' as they came to be called to distinguish them from the new colonists of the Tudor period. The bulk of them refused to accept the reformation and so far they had a common ground with the vast majority of the native Irish. Over much of the country this did a great deal to encourage a fusion of the two groups; but the Old English of the Pale, to whom the natives had always been the enemy, were traditionally loyal to the English connection; and this loyalty survived almost unimpaired through the reign of Elizabeth. But, elsewhere, a slowly growing national sentiment came to be identified with the cause of the papacy; and when the material interests as well as the religious freedom of the Old English were threatened in the reign of Charles I even those of the Pale were ready, though not without reservations, to throw in their lot with the majority.

Elizabeth and Ireland

Religious differences have played such an influential part in Irish politics during the last three and a half centuries that there has been a natural tendency to exaggerate the immediate political results of the reformation. The truth is that the basic continuity of Tudor policy was not affected by the change. Its great object, surviving all ecclesiastical fluctuations, was to make sure that Ireland should not become a centre of intrigue for English rebels or continental enemies. Despite the fact that it issued in military conquest Tudor policy in Ireland was essentially defensive.

Elizabeth succeeded to the throne at a moment when the danger from Ireland seemed particularly acute. Sussex warned her how easy it would be for a foreign power 'aided by civil faction' to get a footing in the country, and prophesied that the result would be 'such a ruin to England as I am afeard to think on'. But shortage of money and the precariousness of her position at home compelled Elizabeth to act cautiously. Fortunately for her, France was too deeply concerned in Scottish affairs to pay much attention to Ireland, and Philip of Spain was still disposed to be conciliatory. This easing of the tension enabled Elizabeth to play a waiting game. The chief source of unrest was in Ulster, where the settlement made by Henry VIII had completely broken down. Conn O'Neill, earl of Tyrone, died in 1559 and the Irish, ignoring the English title and English law of succession, elected his younger son, Shane, as 'The O'Neill'. This was a plain defiance of royal authority, but the government had not the resources necessary for direct military action. Negotiations with Shane went on for years. But though he paid a visit to England and made public submission to the queen, he returned to Ireland as free as he left it and continued to rule in virtual independence. For the time being, the government allowed the Tyrone earldom to lapse.

Shane O'Neill was one of the last of the great Gaelic chieftains. He was a courageous soldier but not a great commander, a clever negotiator, but a short-sighted diplomat; his conception of government was purely personal and his ambition was limited to the establishment of the military supremacy of the O'Neills in Ulster. It was the reckless pursuit of this ambition which led to his downfall. His two main rivals were the O'Donnells of Tyrconnell and the Scottish settlers, MacDonnells from the western isles, who had been for some time establishing themselves in north-east Ulster. The government took advantage of this rivalry to turn O'Neill against the Scots and O'Donnell against O'Neill. For some years Shane was unexpectedly victorious, but in 1567 he was completely overthrown by the O'Donnells. The Scots, to whom he fled for refuge, killed him and sent his head to the deputy. This sudden reversal presented an opportunity which Elizabeth refused to take; once the immediate danger from Ulster was gone she fell back on a policy of defence. Shane's cousin and tanist, Turlough, was allowed to succeed him in peace, with formal recognition as 'chief of his name and nation'. He was an unadventurous ruler, satisfied to hold on quietly to what he had, and though a couple of years later the Irish parliament passed an act of attainder against Shane and confiscated his lands, Turlough was, in fact, left alone. The only important step which the government took was the establishment of Hugh O'Neill, Conn's grandson and the claimant to the earldom of Tyrone, in part of the O'Neill lands, with his father's title of baron of Dungannon (Hugh's father, Matthew, though illegitimate, had been recognized by Henry VIII as Conn's heir, and had been created baron of Dungannon). Hugh's ambition went far beyond this but adversity had taught him caution and infinite patience; for more than twenty years he watched and waited, and when, at last, he threw all on the fortunes of war it was rather to defend what he held than in the hope of making any fresh conquest.

Ulster was cut off from the rest of the country by a natural barrier of mountain and lake and its remoteness discouraged European intervention. So long as the northern chiefs were quiescent it was safe enough to leave them alone. But Munster presented a different sort of problem. Contacts with the Pale were much closer, and the great Anglo-Irish lords who dominated much of the province were uneasy at the government's ecclesiastical policy, cautiously carried out though it was. Above all, the southern ports were in regular communication with Europe and offered easy entry to England's continental enemies. In these circumstances it was a matter of mere necessity to establish effective control over Munster. This might have been accomplished with no more than sporadic resistance had it not been for the determined character of one man, James FitzMaurice FitzGerald (usually referred to as James FitzMaurice), cousin of the earl of Desmond and the most able representative of the Munster Geraldines. The relative importance of the family had been increased by the overthrow of the Kildare branch, but the nominal head of it at this time, Gerald, the fifteenth earl, was a man of weak character, untrustworthy, oppressive and selfishly ambitious, without the strength of will to pursue any consistent policy. In 1567 he was arrested and sent over to England, and James FitzMaurice was left to look after his interests. FitzMaurice was a fanatical opponent of protestantism and of the English government, and it was his aim to build up a Roman Catholic alliance among the Irish and Anglo-Irish of Munster.

Religious motives alone would hardly have produced a rebellion; but every land-holder in Munster was alarmed, at this time, for the security of his title; despite the settlement made by Henry VIII, long-dormant claims were being revived by litigants who enjoyed the support of the government and whom the judges were likely to favour. FitzMaurice played upon these fears, and the detention of Desmond in England seemed to justify suspicion of the government's honesty. In these circumstances he gained many supporters and began his revolt in the summer of 1569. His own enthusiasm gave it something of the character of a crusade, an aspect which he naturally stressed in his appeals to the pope and to the king of Spain. The publication, early in 1570, of the papal bull *Regnans in excelsis* (in which Pope Pius V declared Elizabeth excommunicate and her subjects released from their obedience) may have increased the religious zeal of the rebels, but it brought them no practical aid and it complicated their political position. The king of Spain sent a small supply of arms, but no men and little money. Within a short time the military successes of the English enabled them to take effective measures for the restoration of order. The most important step in this direction was the establishment of a new system of government for Munster. A president was appointed with extensive authority over the province and with a council and court of his own. The first president, Sir John Perrot, fought and governed vigorously. He soon deprived FitzMaurice of effective control over any extensive territory and in January 1572 compelled him to submit.

As in Ulster, once the immediate threat had been averted the government relaxed its efforts. Desmond was allowed to retain his earldom and to return to Ireland, and FitzMaurice was set at liberty. But the relaxation was more apparent than real, for Perrot continued to work effectively for the establishment of English law and it was clear that the old semi-independence of the Munster lords was drawing to an end. FitzMaurice did not abandon his intrigues, but soon realized that nothing could be accomplished without foreign aid. In 1575 he escaped to the continent where he spent his time 'running from one papist prince to another with the pope's commendations' and trying to gather an army for the invasion of Ireland. At length, in 1579, he landed at Dingle with a mixed force of some 300 Italians and Spaniards financed by the pope and the king of Spain. With him came Nicholas Sanders, an Englishman, as papal nuncio, whose presence emphasized still further the religious aspect of the undertaking, upon which FitzMaurice had from the start laid so much stress.

The war that followed was not one of battles but of skirmishes, ambushes and sieges. Elizabeth would not afford either men or money to make a speedy end, nor did the nature of the country make such a policy easy. The rebels were constantly sustained, despite reverses, by the hope of Spanish help. But when help did come, in November 1580, it proved of little use. A force of 600 Spaniards landed at Smerwick, fortified the town and waited to see what would happen. The rebels were just as dilatory; but the deputy, Lord Grey de Wilton, acted at once. He assembled every man he could spare, marched against Smerwick, compelled the Spaniards to surrender at discretion and put them all to the sword. But this very success helped to prolong the war; for Elizabeth, convinced that no more Spanish troops would be sent, cut down supplies and left the deputy to bring the war to a lingering end with reduced forces. The fighting dragged on for another three years and almost all Munster was laid waste. The cruelties committed by both sides were such as naturally occur in a struggle between an organized army and elusive guerilla forces which have the sympathy of the countryside and which cannot or will not fight pitched battles. Both sides suffered from shortage of supplies, but the rebels also lacked effective leadership. FitzMaurice was killed in a skirmish with the Burkes a month after his landing; he was succeeded by Sir John of Desmond, the earl's brother, who was killed in 1581, and in the same year Sanders died of hunger and dysentery. The earl of Desmond himself, without plan or principle, could do little to hold his supporters together; but the prestige of his position counted for something, and his death in November 1583 was the signal for general submission. The Munster rebellion was over.

The religious aspect of the rebellion was significant, for it marked a step towards the union of native Irish and Old English against the government on the basis of their common faith. Such a union was never completely accomplished, and at this stage long-standing racial and family rivalries often counted for more than religious affinities. In Munster not only the Butlers and their allies but many of the native Irish remained loyal to the queen. In the Pale, and in the Anglo-Irish towns throughout the country, though there was some sympathy with the rebels, loyalty was the rule. But the general effect of the war was to sharpen the political barrier between protestantism and Roman Catholicism and to strengthen the government's conviction that the latter was synonymous with treason. It was this conviction that prepared the way for a systematic politico-religious persecution in the next century.

Though Elizabeth had been forced into the Munster war by the need for guarding Ireland against invasion, her own policy had already made an armed clash with the old order almost inevitable. Henry VIII, faced with hostility both at home and abroad, had embarked on a policy of anglicization, and his successors had little choice but to follow his example. But every strengthening of royal authority, every extension of English law, however necessary to the security of the kingdom, was a threat to their independence which the Irish and Anglo-Irish magnates were almost bound to resist. In these circumstances Henry's system of 'surrender and re-grant' broke down, and in Mary's reign the first experiment was made in establishing 'plantations'. Mary's plantations were in Leix and Offaly, renamed Queen's County and King's County, and though they failed the idea was not abandoned. A new attempt in Ulster, after the formal confiscation of Shane O'Neill's lands, was costly, but no more successful. In spite of this, the government decided to take the opportunity presented by the end of the Munster rebellion to embark on an even more elaborate scheme. England was beginning to feel the need of an outlet for her population, and the idea of such organized plantations, combining state direction with private enterprise, seems to have appealed to the Tudor mind. The various Irish projects of this and the succeeding century are linked with the general movement towards overseas expansion; that which Burghley and Walsingham drew up for Munster was based in part upon Raleigh's proposals for Virginia, and Raleigh himself, his half-brother Sir Humphrey Gilbert, with others of less note, were engaged in plantation enterprises both in Ireland and America.

In Ireland the main object of the plantation policy was to substitute loyal English settlers for disloyal Irish or Anglo-Irish. About 400,000 acres of land confiscated after the Munster rebellion was to be divided into 'seignories', varying in size from 4000 to 12,000 acres. These were to be granted to English 'undertakers' who were to plant them with English-born families. The management of the whole affair was incompetent and slow, the necessary surveying was inaccurately done and years passed between the making of grants and the actual establishment of the grantees in possession. A commission of inquiry in 1592 found that of fifty-eight undertakers only thirteen were resident and that there were only 245 English families on the planted lands. This comparative failure was due partly to incompetence, partly to the readiness with which undertakers, anxious for quick returns, accepted Irish tenants at high rents, in spite of their agreement to bring in English. But an even more important reason was the havoc which three or four years of warfare had produced in Munster. Famine and disease, as well as war, had depopulated the country, and the new settlement was scarcely beginning to be profitable when it was practically swept away in the insurrection of 1598.

Four years later, when Raleigh sold his Munster estate of 42,000 acres it was said to be costing him £200 a year in upkeep.

Though Elizabeth was ready, when occasion offered, to follow Mary's policy of military conquest secured by plantation, she was also ready to continue and adapt her father's more peaceful methods. It was in this way that she set about extending effective royal authority over Connaught. In 1585 a commission was appointed to report on the rights and holdings of all the Anglo-Irish and Irish lords and chiefs of the province, and on the basis of this report a settlement was made. Each landholder was confirmed in his estate, with a new title good in English law, and in return was to pay a quit-rent to the crown. Existing feudal and Irish services due from tenant to lord were abolished and money rents substituted. Old Irish family titles, such as 'O'Connor Don' and 'O'Connor Sligo', were prohibited. Succession by primogeniture was established. Connaught thus escaped the plantation policy that affected, to a greater or lesser degree, the other three provinces; but though the people remained undisturbed, the Gaelic way of life, so closely bound up with personal services and with family rather than territorial titles, was seriously undermined. This 'composition of Connaught' was to have been confirmed in parliament, but this was not done; and later, in the reign of Charles I, Wentworth was able to call the whole settlement in question.

Thus, by a combination of force and diplomacy, and urged on by fear rather than ambition, Elizabeth extended her authority over a wider area of Ireland than had been effectively controlled by any previous English sovereign. The medieval administrative system was expanded and modified to meet the new situation. Old counties were revived and new ones established. By 1585 almost all Ireland outside Ulster had been reduced to shire ground, and even Ulster had been shired on paper. The presidency system, which had now been established in Connaught as well as in Munster, performed much the same function as the English Council of the North and Council of Wales. The court of Castle Chamber in Dublin dealt with the same sort of cases as the court of Star Chamber in England. But the similarity between the English and Irish governmental systems was not so close as this comparison might suggest. The English government was of natural growth and rested upon the implicit consent of the people; in Ireland the very notion of effective central authority had been imposed from outside, the independence of local magnates had still to be reckoned with, and government relied directly upon military force.

The difference in spirit between the two systems becomes clear when we consider the part played by the Irish parliament. Throughout Elizabeth's reign it met only three times in all. The first of these meetings, in 1560, was concerned almost exclusively with the ecclesiastical settlement and lasted for less than three weeks. The second parliament, in 1569, was that which attainted Shane O'Neill. Here, for the first time, two parties emerge fairly clearly: the government or 'court' party, consisting mainly of officials and of nominees of the deputy, returned by counties, cities and boroughs under royal control, and an opposition party made up of Anglo-Irish gentry. The life of this parliament was brief and the struggle between the parties did not come to a head over any major issue; but the government was uneasy at the strength of the opposition and did not call parliament again until 1585, when it was felt desirable to have acts of attainder passed against the leaders of the Munster rebellion. The membership of the lower house in this parliament reflected the expansion of royal power: there were members from twenty-seven counties and thirty-six cities and boroughs, so that, territorially at least, almost the whole kingdom was represented; but a racial exclusiveness remained, for the members were almost without exception English by birth or descent, either new settlers or old colonists. Once again, two parties emerged and the line of division was now clearly religious. The opposition was made up of 'recusants' (i.e. those who refused to take the oath of supremacy) and was strong enough to defeat proposed government legislation against the Jesuits. But most of the other measures put forward by the government, including the acts of attainder, got through. Despite this degree of success Elizabeth did not summon the Irish parliament again.

This brief account of the Irish parliament under Elizabeth suggests three comments. First, it was called only to deal with special topics and formed no regular part of the governmental system. Secondly, it was essentially a 'loyal' body: the opposition attacked certain aspects of government policy, but they stood fast by the authority of the English crown and were quite ready to attaint rebels. Thirdly, the existence of a constitutional opposition, though it was a check on the government, was a step towards establishing general peace: if all the opposition elements in the country could be drawn within the parliamentary system they would no longer be a threat to peace and security. But events showed that this could not be brought about save by an extension of military conquest.

Hugh O'Neill and the end of Gaelic resistance

During the ten years which followed the end of the Munster war Ireland enjoyed an unwonted peace. The power and prestige of the government expanded. The danger of Spanish intervention was at least checked by the overthrow of the armada in 1588. The established church showed signs of more vigorous life, and the setting up of a university in Dublin (Trinity College) in 1591 promised a more plentiful supply of well-trained and zealous clergy. At no previous point had the progressive anglicization of the whole country seemed so likely. In retrospect, one can see that the very prospect of such a development might well bring on a struggle with Ulster, the last important stronghold of Gaelic tradition; but, at the time, the position in Ulster seemed safe enough. The government's protégé, Hugh O'Neill, who was steadily building up his influence, maintained at least a formal loyalty. He had served in person against the Munster rebels and he had attended the parliament of 1585, in which his claim to the earldom of Tyrone had been recognized. A couple of years later he had received further grants of land from the queen. Yet it was round Hugh O'Neill that the opposition of Ulster, and most of Ireland, was to gather.

Hugh was more subtle and more far-sighted than his uncle Shane, but his outlook was not essentially different. He was an O'Neill: his first ambition was to secure recognition as 'chief of his name and nation' and thereafter to establish O'Neill supremacy in Ulster. But he realized, as Shane had never done, the need for caution. Instead of defying his cousin Turlough, Shane's successor, he persuaded him to give up his position peaceably, and in 1593 Hugh himself took the title of 'The O'Neill'. Instead of trying to crush all rival powers in the north he made a firm alliance with the chief of the O'Donnells, Hugh Roe. Both actions were alarming to the government, for the native title was, strictly speaking, illegal, and Hugh Roe O'Donnell was strongly anti-English. It need not be supposed, however, that O'Neill's previous professions of loyalty were entirely insincere. He was quite prepared to be loyal so long as his loyalty did not clash with his personal ambition. But if he was to be recognized by his countrymen as chief of his name he must take the traditional title. To be 'earl of Tyrone' meant very little in Ulster; to be 'The O'Neill' meant almost everything. Again, he must either fight Hugh Roe or make friends with him, and there can be no doubt about the wisdom of his choice. He was not preparing for aggression, but merely for the defence of what he considered his rights. And the need for such defence seemed to be increasing. Although the government had not deliberately embarked on a complete conquest it was becoming clear that anglicization could not stop short at the borders of Ulster. Already in 1591 a land settlement in Monaghan, similar to that in Connaught, had undermined the traditional way of life there. The establishment of military garrisons at various strategic points suggested that the ground was being prepared for a general assault upon the north.

The truth is that both sides acted out of fear. The government was alarmed at the growing power and independence of O'Neill and could not ignore the possibility of a new Spanish attack, with Ulster instead of Munster as its first object. O'Neill and O'Donnell saw the Gaelic tradition being gradually eaten away in the rest of Ireland and they looked forward with dismay to the prospect of English law and the reformed church being imposed upon Ulster also. The lament of a southern bard over the fallen state of the O'Byrnes reflects the natural horror of an aristocratic society at the levelling tendency of the English legal system:

Torment it is to me that in the very tribal gatherings foreigners proscribe them that are Ireland's royal chiefs, in whose own ancestral territory is vouchsafed them now no designation other than the lowly wood-kerne's name.*

In this uneasy position casual armed clashes led naturally to a general struggle. There was some desultory fighting in 1594, in which O'Donnell and some of the lesser chiefs were involved. In the following spring Hugh O'Neill himself took the field. The war which followed soon acquired something of a national character, but it began because Hugh O'Neill felt that his position in Ulster was threatened.

The government made the initial mistake of supposing that Hugh could be dealt with as easily as Shane had been, and that the alliance of the northern chiefs would soon break up. They were therefore ready to make terms and to follow delaying tactics, believing that time was in their favour. But Hugh's position became stronger instead of weaker, and in August 1598 the whole situation was changed by his crushing defeat of the English commander, Sir Henry Bagenal, at the battle of the Yellow Ford. The effects of the battle were felt throughout Ireland. In Connaught, the Burkes now joined the rebels; in Munster, a general insurrection swept away

*S. H. O'Grady, *Catalogue of Irish MSS in the British Museum*, vol. 1, p. 505.

almost every trace of the recent plantation; throughout Leinster even on the borders of the Pale, the native Irish – the O'Connors, the O'Mores, the O'Byrnes, and the rest – rose in revolt. The battle of the Yellow Ford threatened to turn an Ulster insurrection into a national war in which the bond of a common religion would link Irish and Anglo-Irish under the elected leader of the most illustrious of the ancient royal houses of Ireland.

But the position was neither so simple nor so favourable for O'Neill as might at first appear. Some of the native Irish rulers still held to the crown. In Munster, though an earl of Desmond was found to revive the claims and alliances of his family, Ormond stood fast, a centre of loyal resistance. The towns, both in the Pale and throughout the south and west, remained loyal to the government. Once O'Neill ventured out of Ulster they were a constant menace to his communications and they made it impossible for him or his allies to establish a firm grip on the country. Above all, the lords and gentry of the Pale, though recusants for the most part, continued to support the crown. But the weaknesses in O'Neill's position were not immediately obvious and the government was shaken out of its usual complacency by the magnitude of the danger. An Ireland under Spanish control would threaten the whole structure of English power, based as it was upon command of the sea. From this time onwards men and money were poured into Ireland on an unprecedented scale and the policy of petty economies and makeshift expedients was abandoned.

Almost as soon as the news of O'Neill's victory and its results reached England the government there set to work to prepare a new army. The command was entrusted to the earl of Essex and in April 1599 he arrived in Ireland with almost 20,000 men. But though Essex was a good soldier he had not the qualities necessary for Irish warfare. He frittered away his resources and instead of attacking O'Neill at once allowed him to negotiate. Essex's failure led directly to his own downfall and he was replaced by a commander of a different stamp – Charles Blount, Lord Mountjoy. Mountjoy arrived in Ireland with a carefully worked-out plan of campaign which was eventually to bring O'Neill to destruction. He resolved to avoid pitched battles, to strengthen existing garrisons and establish new ones, to destroy crops and cattle, to cut off O'Neill's sources of supply, and so to wear him out. It is a method by which well-equipped and well-supplied forces have rarely failed to defeat an irregular enemy, however courageous; and on this occasion, though success came slowly, it came surely. The first great blow to O'Neill was the establishment of a fort at Derry. This could be maintained by sea and it was a constant threat to his rear; from Derry, also, other garrisons were planted throughout the north and thus his communications, even within his own country, were endangered.

O'Neill's position was now a precarious one. He had gained no permanent advantage from his great victory of 1598, for the insurrections in Munster and Connaught had flickered out. He could not maintain himself indefinitely in Ulster, the time for negotiation had passed, and his one chance lay in the arrival of substantial foreign help. But when help did come it proved useless. In September 1601 a Spanish fleet, with 4000 troops on board, reached Kinsale. They received little reinforcement from the neighbouring population, they made no attempt to advance inland, and were soon closely besieged by an English army. Three years earlier, in the first flush of the victory of the Yellow Ford, the arrival of such a force might have turned the scale; now, it offered no more than a last desperate hope. O'Neill and O'Donnell marched south with all the troops they could raise. They encamped near Kinsale and established communications with the Spaniards; but an attempt at combined action, which was meant to take the English by surprise, failed completely and the Irish were heavily defeated. O'Neill retreated to the north, O'Donnell took ship for Spain, and the Spaniards surrendered Kinsale on terms which left them free to return home. The war dragged on for more than a year longer; but O'Neill, forced back finally on Ulster and deprived of his allies, was fighting now for terms, not for victory.

Elizabeth did not live to see the end. O'Neill's final submission, in March 1603, took place six days after her death; and it was James I who settled the conditions upon which the defeated chiefs were to live. In appearance, these were generous enough. At the time of his submission O'Neill had given up his native title and abjured foreign alliances; James allowed him to retain the earldom of Tyrone and confirmed him in most of the lands granted to his grandfather Conn in 1542. Rory, younger brother of Hugh O'Donnell, was made earl of Tyrconnell. Other chiefs who had been in rebellion were given similar terms according to their rank. There were no stipulations about religion. In form, the settlement differed little from others made or proposed at various stages during the long struggle between Tudor England and the Irish kings; and many of those who had suffered in the cause of government complained that O'Neill had got more by rebellion than they by loyalty. But in fact O'Neill was beaten. Generous terms were possible because he was no longer dangerous and his inactivity during the next few years shows that he knew it. What he still held he held by grace of the king and not in his own strength.

With the surrender of Hugh O'Neill the Tudor conquest was complete. The social and political system of Gaelic Ireland was gone; the traditional authority of the chief and the rights assured under the brehon law were replaced by the authority of the Dublin government and the common law of England. Gaelic society was aristocratic: it was the chiefs and their privileged dependants who suffered most from the change and whose downfall fills the laments of the professional bards. For the labouring population the new order may well have been in some respects beneficial; but there was little likelihood that they would become reconciled to it. The Gaelic language long survived the destruction of the Gaelic social system, keeping alive the traditions of the past, and setting a barrier between the mass of the population and their new rulers. It was even more important that the religious distinction had by this time become stable; and though Mountjoy's victories enabled the reformed church to expand its authority in the north there was little or no change in the ecclesiastical allegiance of the people. Despite its military completeness, the Tudor conquest left a foundation for continuing resistance to English power.

During the long-drawn-out wars of conquest the country had been systematically wasted by both sides, and contemporary accounts give a very gloomy picture of Ireland at the end of Elizabeth's reign. But Irish rural economy, perhaps because it was simple, had the power of rapid recovery, and wealth increased during the peaceful period which followed the accession of James I. The political changes brought about by conquest had, however, a permanent effect on the economic life of the country. Up to the middle of the sixteenth century a great part of Ireland's commercial wealth was concentrated in the ports of the south and west, which traded with the continent, and especially with Spain. Some of them, Galway above all, maintained a virtual independence of the crown, though their populations were largely English, or Anglo-Norman, in blood and tradition. Now, with royal authority extending over the whole kingdom, their former freedom was gone; and though their overseas trade did not disappear, the tightening of the English connection naturally increased the relative importance of Dublin and Drogheda and the other ports on the east coast, well placed as they were for commerce with England. This increasing Anglo-Irish trade formed one of the main supports of the 'New English' interest which was establishing itself in Ireland and which was to play a significant part in the civil strife of the mid seventeenth century.

3 The seventeenth century

The early Stuarts

With the accession of James I Irish history entered upon a new phase. The last centre of Gaelic particularism had been destroyed and the whole country lay open for the firm establishment of royal authority – the 'kingdom of Ireland' had at last become a reality. Various factors seemed to promise peace and well-being. The union of England, Scotland and Ireland under one crown secured a greater degree of stability in the politics of the British Isles. James showed that he did not mean to press the English victory beyond the point of necessary security: not only were O'Neill and O'Donnell confirmed in their estates but an act of oblivion removed the fear that prosecutions against former rebels might be renewed. The conclusion of peace with Spain in 1604 helped the development of overseas trade, while the increasingly effective enforcement of internal order provided one of the necessary conditions of prosperity at home. The outlook for English power in Ireland and for the general economic improvement of the country seemed brighter in 1603 than for centuries before. But a generation later these pleasing prospects were destroyed in the insurrection of 1641.

The failure of the early Stuart monarchy in Ireland has sometimes been attributed to the tyranny or mismanagement of Wentworth, and sometimes to the internal complications of English politics. But its roots ran far into the past, and the final breach between Charles I and the English parliament was the result and not the cause of insurrection in Ireland. The truth is that the completion of the conquest had simply transferred from the military to the political sphere the great problems of Irish government and of Anglo-Irish relations; but since in the circumstances of the early seventeenth century a political solution of these problems was almost unattainable the renewal of war could hardly be avoided. The difficulties with which Charles I had to contend in Great Britain and the nature of Wentworth's government in Ireland undoubtedly affected the course of events, but could not alter the general pattern. That pattern was mainly determined by the internal conflict of interests which the previous history of Ireland had produced, complicated by those problems of religion and land which in one form or another were to vex Irish political life for centuries to come.

At the beginning of the seventeenth century native Irish chiefs, though deprived of political independence, still held a considerable proportion of the country as landlords by English law. The Old English had a dominant position among the nobles and gentry of Leinster and Munster, and in most of the cities and boroughs. These two groups were mainly Roman Catholic, and together they formed the bulk of the landowning and trading classes. But there was also an English population of more recent settlement, made up largely of government officials and their dependants, who had already acquired a good deal of landed property and were constantly on the alert for more. They were mainly if not exclusively protestant and formed the backbone of the established church. The government naturally desired to enlarge this element in the population and for this purpose revived and extended the sixteenth-century policy of plantation.

The most extensive and by far the most successful effort in this direction was the plantation in Ulster. The opportunity was provided by the event always known in Irish history as 'the flight of the earls'. The 'earls' were Tyrone and Tyrconnell, who had never become reconciled to the position in which the war against Elizabeth had left them. Though established in vast estates they could not but feel that their real power was gone with their Irish titles and their political independence. They suspected, with some justice, that many influential government officials were hostile to them and jealous of the liberal treatment they had received. But whether they feared the effect of this hostility on their position in Ireland or hoped to gain foreign help for a renewal of the struggle does not appear. All that is certain is that they secretly obtained a ship and left Ireland in September 1607 with a considerable body of their allies and dependants. They received a scant welcome and no help on the continent, until they came to Rome, and they made no effort at any military adventure. But their going left the greater part of Ulster open to confiscation, and the government resolved to seize the opportunity. The secret departure of the earls was regarded as evidence of treason, and the whole area over which they had exercised or claimed lordship was declared forfeit to the crown. This area consisted of the six counties of Armagh, Cavan, Coleraine (now Londonderry), Donegal,

Fermanagh, Tyrone. Most, but not all, of the native landlords who had held under Tyrone or Tyrconnell were deprived of their estates. Great areas were handed over to English and Scots 'undertakers' on condition that they planted their estates with British settlers. Other areas went to 'servitors', men who had served the crown in Ireland, who were allowed to take Irish as well as British tenants; and the same liberty applied also to the extensive church lands. There was thus a general change in the ownership of land; but contrary to the government's intention, there was no large-scale removal of the native population. In each of the planted counties there were certain areas from which, according to the plantation scheme, the natives were to be removed completely, but in fact this was never done. The difficulty of bringing in English and Scots made the new owners quite ready to ignore the conditions imposed by the government and accept the existing occupants, some of whom, of course, were the former landlords, as their tenants. A great share in the settlement was taken by the corporation of London, after which the county and city of Londonderry are named; and the direct interest in Irish affairs which London thus acquired helped to complicate its relations with the crown in the reign of Charles I. The progress of the plantation was slow, but the foundations were more firmly laid than in the Munster plantation of Elizabeth's reign, and the steady infiltration of colonists, and especially of lowland Scots, gradually built up a British and protestant population in the north. By 1628, however, there were only about 2000 British families in the six planted counties.

The two counties of Antrim and Down were not included in the general confiscation, but considerable parts of them had been taken into the king's hands on other grounds and granted to various English and Scottish settlers, even before the main plantation had been begun. In this way the families of Hill, Montgomery and Hamilton, with many others of less note, established themselves in north-east Ulster, and laid the foundations of the strong Anglo-Scottish protestantism which is still characteristic of the area. The older Scottish settlers, the MacDonnells, were confirmed in their lands in north Antrim; but their traditions were Roman Catholic and Gaelic, and they did not mingle readily with their new neighbours.

These plantations were to have an enduring influence on the social and political life of Ulster. In their more immediate effect they introduced into the province an element of unrest that contributed materially to the insurrection of 1641. The Irish chiefs who had gone into exile and those who had subsequently been dispossessed in the course of the plantation had maintained considerable personal body-guards, for whom no provision was now made. Sir Arthur Chichester, the deputy, realized the danger presented by these 'swordsmen' and had some hundreds of them shipped off to Sweden to serve in the armies of Charles IX; but many more eluded capture and together with some of the dispossessed proprietors, who disdained to live as tenants on their former estates, they took shelter in the woods and hills, lived on the plunder of the countryside and kept alive the memory of the past until the time should come for striking another blow against the English power.

The Old English were not affected by the confiscations in Ulster. Their main grievance at the beginning of James's reign was religious, and their hope of improving their position was encouraged by the general ineffectiveness of the established church. The Elizabethan conquest had been accompanied by some efforts to carry out the acts of supremacy and uniformity. The Munster plantation, for example, had included plans for the establishment of protestant clergy in the parishes. But, despite this, contemporary accounts give a most gloomy picture of the state of affairs: the churches in ruins, ecclesiastical incomes turned to secular uses, the parochial clergy absentees or grossly incompetent, the bishops greedy pluralists, the people either abandoned to heathenism, with 'no more demonstration of religion than amongst Tartars or cannibals', or left to the ministra-tion of the Roman Catholic clergy, who, undeterred by danger and poverty, flocked into the country from continental seminaries. Even in the Pale there were often no churches for the people to attend, so that those who were willing to conform could not do so. While the reformed church showed so little sense of its responsibilities and made so little use of its advantages it was natural that the Roman Catholics, fortified by their numbers and encouraged by the zeal of their clergy, should not rest satisfied with an ecclesiastical settlement that placed their enemies in possession of the machinery and endow-ments of the church. The accession of James I seemed to provide just such an opportunity as they had been waiting for. While king of Scotland he had been in communication with O'Neill and O'Donnell, he was supposed to be sympathetic towards his mother's faith and there was a general belief in Ireland that he would at least establish a legal toleration. Acting on these hopes the magistrates of Water-ford, Kilkenny, Cork, Limerick and other of the southern towns seized the churches and handed them over to the Roman Catholic clergy. Though some show of force on the part of the deputy soon restored order, the incident was a clear indication of the kind of problem that James would have to face. But in fact, neither James nor Charles would ever face the problem squarely; they would neither enforce the law as it stood nor establish a legal toleration. Frequent but ineffective proclamations against the Roman Catholics and occasional acts of severity prevented them from having any sense either of security or of gratitude; while the church of Ireland, though somewhat improved in discipline, could make little headway against their zealous and efficient clergy, whom the government seemed powerless to expel or control.

From the government's point of view the chief danger was that the religious sympathy between Irish and Old English would lead to political alliance. Since the reign of Elizabeth the common title of 'recusant' had been applied to all who refused the oath of supremacy, irrespective of their race; but divergent traditions of loyalty and difference of interest were still strong. The Old English recusants, unlike the native Irish, occupied a strong constitutional position, as appeared in the parliament which James called in 1613, partly to ratify the Ulster plantation, partly to secure some increase of revenue. The government had made careful preparations, including the creation of forty new boroughs, and when parliament met at Dublin in 1613 there was a considerable protestant majority. The recusants, who represented the wealth and property of the Old English, withdrew in protest, and the moral effect of this was so great that the government dared not proceed in their absence. Parliament was prorogued so that an inquiry could be made into their grievances; and so many elections were disallowed that when it met again in October 1614 the protestant majority had been reduced to a very narrow margin. As a result, the government had to abandon legislation it had proposed against the Jesuits. But the other measures passed by this parliament, including acts for the recognition of the king's title and for the attainder of Tyrone and Tyrconnell, showed that the secular loyalty of the recusants was still unimpaired. Nevertheless, the general outcome was unsatisfactory to the government. Not only had the recusants won a moral victory, but very little had been done to increase the revenue; and in Ireland as in England Stuart governments were perpetually short of money. To remedy both these defects – to ensure an adequate protestant majority in future parliaments and to increase the income of the crown – James

A.S.H.O.I.–C

decided to push on more vigorously with the policy of plantation.

The basis of the new plantation policy was the revival of dormant royal claims. In 1615 the crown lawyers began an attack upon the titles of landlords in the county of Wexford and within the next few years similar attacks were made in Longford, King's County, Leitrim and elsewhere. It was an easy thing to find flaws in the title to an Irish estate, and it was seldom difficult to persuade or bully a jury into giving a verdict for the crown. There was no intention of wholesale dispossession; where the king's claim succeeded, a proportion of the land, usually one quarter, was set aside for plantation, and the rest regranted to the former occupant. This process certainly resulted in some pecuniary profit to the crown, for a fine had to be paid for the new title and a rent was reserved on the land. But the plantation part of the scheme came to very little. Estates were granted to undertakers, many of whom never visited the country, and who were in general content to make what profit they could out of the existing holders.

This policy produced general uneasiness throughout the kingdom during the later years of James I. No one felt safe: the new plantations affected the Old English as well as the native Irish; and even the English and Scottish planters in Ulster found themselves threatened with penalties for their failure to carry out strictly the terms of their undertakings. And there were other causes of grievance. James found the regular revenue, even when supplemented by income from plantation schemes, quite unequal to the cost of government; he was unwilling to risk another parliament, and in 1622 set up a court of wards, mainly for the sake of the financial profit. The use of the court as a means of proselytizing, by entrusting the education of Roman Catholic minors to protestant guardians, naturally aroused the hostility of the recusants.

The seriousness both of the unrest in the country and of the poverty of the government was increased by the break with Spain in 1624. It was obviously necessary to secure Ireland against a possible attack and to minimize the chance of a pro-Spanish insurrection. The general interests of England were so deeply involved in this that the English parliament voted a large sum for the defence of Ireland. The war with Spain was followed, early in the reign of Charles I, by war with France; the English parliament was not now so ready to assist the king, and it was therefore more than ever necessary that the revenue of Ireland should be increased. Out of these circumstances rose the idea of a bargain between the king and the Irish landlords, the king offering certain concessions in return for immediate financial help. After many months of discussion terms were agreed in May 1628: land-holders were not to be disturbed by royal claims based on titles more than sixty years old, and special guarantees were given for titles in Ulster and Connaught; the enforcement of the oath of supremacy was to be relaxed in certain cases; in return, the king was to have £120000, paid over three years. It was intended that a parliament should meet to confirm these royal concessions (the 'Graces'), and the money paid in return for them was to be deducted from any subsidies granted by the parliament. In fact, however, the proposal to summon parliament was dropped; and the 'Graces', having no legal sanction, rested solely on the king's will.

Falkland, the deputy who had helped to negotiate the bargain of 1628, was recalled in the following year. He was an unpopular and not very successful ruler, but his immediate successors were a great deal worse. Charles did not at once appoint another deputy, but entrusted the government to two lords justices, Richard Boyle, earl of Cork, and Adam Loftus, the lord chancellor. Both were representatives of the new English interest established in Ireland during the reign of Elizabeth; they were able men, though greedy of gain, but their mutual hostility, apart from other difficulties, made efficient government impossible. In ecclesiastical affairs they were hampered by doubt about what the king really intended. Strict enforcement of the acts of uniformity and supremacy could not be expected, but protestant opinion in both kingdoms was alarmed at the open activity of the Jesuits and the establishment of religious houses, even in Dublin itself. Occasional attempts at suppression had no effect but to excite the anger of the recusants. To counter possible danger the lords justices had increased the army, but they had no money to pay it and the soldiers lived at free quarters on the country. The war with Spain had cut off one important part of Ireland's overseas trade, and the rest was seriously hampered by pirates, especially the Algerines, who were even strong enough to sack the port of Baltimore in 1631. Ireland seemed to be drifting into general confusion at the very time when Charles, who was now attempting to rule England without a parliament, was most in need of help. It was in these circumstances that the king decided to appoint as lord deputy Sir Thomas Wentworth, who had already rendered him good service as president of the council of the north. Wentworth arrived in Dublin in 1633 and from then until his final departure in 1640 he ruled Ireland sternly, in some respects unscrupulously, but on the whole more efficiently than she had ever been ruled before.

There was little in Wentworth's policy that was new, except the thoroughness with which he carried it out. By 1636 he had gone far towards reforming the worst abuses and disorders in church and state. Ecclesiastical lands and revenues had been recovered, churches rebuilt, clerical residence in some measure enforced, and convocation, though asserting its national independence, had been induced to accept the thirty-nine articles of the church of England. A parliament had been successfully held, and its generous grants had removed a burden of debt and helped to establish the revenue upon a firmer footing; and all this had been gained without any confirmation of the Graces. The coast had been cleared of pirates, trade was improving and the income from customs duties rising steadily. To Wentworth all this was a means to an end. His rule in Ireland must be considered in the light of his general policy; his great object was to break down throughout the British Isles every force which stood against the absolute authority of the crown and he was determined to use the resources of Ireland to strengthen the monarchy in Great Britain. For this reason he spent much of the increased revenue on the army. He paid it regularly, improved its discipline and saw that it was properly equipped. In 1639 he was prepared to use it to enforce the king's authority in Scotland, and the suspicion that he had also advised the king to use it in England strengthened the determination with which the English house of commons was later to insist upon his death.

The same subjection of Ireland to the main design appears in Wentworth's economic policy. The centre of royal power must always be in England and so Ireland must be kept in a dependent condition. He therefore discouraged the woollen industry, not only lest it should interfere with English prosperity, but also in order that Ireland might be forced to depend on England for supplies:

All wisdom advises to keep this kingdom as much subordinate and dependent on England as is possible; and holding them from the manufacture of wool, and thus enforcing them to fetch their clothing from thence . . . how can they depart from us without nakedness and beggary?

At the same time, he promoted the linen manufacture for which Ireland had formerly been famous, but which had declined during the Elizabethan wars, for this did not clash with any English interest.

When Wentworth left Ireland for the last time in April 1640 he declared that the Irish were 'as fully satisfied and as well affected to his majesty's person and service as can possibly be wished for'. This might have seemed true enough on the surface, but his government had done nothing to bring permanent tranquillity into Irish political life; and though it is a mistake to regard Wentworth as mainly responsible for the insurrection of 1641 his policy undoubtedly contributed to the general unrest that showed itself soon after his departure. His refusal to confirm the Graces in parliament left the way open for a renewed attack upon land titles, which he pressed on with unscrupulous vigour. The court of Castle Chamber, the Irish equivalent of the English Star Chamber, was used to overawe juries that refused to find for the crown, and in this way lands were confiscated, fines exacted and rents imposed. The London companies in Ulster, the entire province of Connaught, Elizabethan settlers like the earl of Cork, all had to submit; and the ill-feeling aroused was more than enough to offset the effects of economic prosperity. The recusants enjoyed a great measure of toleration, but for this they had no security and were not likely to become reconciled to a position of permanent inferiority, while the failure to enforce the law against them alarmed and angered the protestants. Wentworth's ecclesiastical reforms, carried out largely under the influence of Laud, tended to alienate the more zealous of the clergy, for the Irish church was still very much affected by the calvinistic theology which was being gradually pushed out of the church of England. Thus almost every powerful interest in the kingdom, though forced into temporary submission, was ready to turn against Wentworth as soon as opportunity should offer. The merchants prospered; the common people were relieved from the burden of a rapacious soldiery and given some protection against brigands and pirates; in cases where crown interests were not concerned the courts administered justice with a strictness that Ireland had rarely known; but all this counted for little in a country dominated by landlords and torn by religious strife.

The situation in Ireland was closely affected by what was happening in Great Britain and this was particularly true of the north-east, which maintained a regular intercourse with Scotland. Here Wentworth's Laudian zeal had provoked another source of discord. The Scottish settlers in Ulster had brought their presbyterianism with them, but so far they had managed to live within the pale of the established church. Some of the northern bishops were Scots, and had allowed their countrymen to occupy livings without too strict an inquiry into their doctrine or any rigid insistence upon the acts of supremacy and uniformity. Such a state of affairs was a scandal to

Laud and Wentworth. John Bramhall, a Yorkshireman who had come to Ireland as Wentworth's chaplain, was appointed to the see of Derry to enforce the discipline of the church. Under his leadership other bishops took similar action, and many ministers who refused to conform returned to Scotland, where they took a leading part in the agitation preceding the national covenant of 1638. But, though a considerable degree of outward conformity was established in Ulster, its insecurity was revealed in 1639. In that year, when war threatened between England and Scotland. Wentworth tried to ensure the loyalty of Ulster by imposing on the Scottish settlers an oath of unconditional obedience to royal commands. The 'black oath', as it was called, was refused by hundreds of people of all ranks; some of them were seized and imprisoned, but great numbers took refuge in the woods and hills, or fled back to Scotland. Thus Wentworth not only added to his own enemies at home and to the king's in Scotland, but he weakened and divided the British and protestant interest in Ulster when it was on the eve of a most dangerous assault.

Insurrection and reconquest, 1641–60

The roots of the Ulster insurrection of 1641 are to be found in the Elizabethan conquest and the plantations of the early seventeenth century; but its outbreak and character were largely determined by contemporary events in Great Britain. The meeting of the Long Parliament was quickly followed by the overthrow of Wentworth (now earl of Strafford), with a consequent weakening of government in Ireland. At the same time, the practical toleration enjoyed by the recusants was threatened by the growing strength of the puritan party in England. Events in Scotland had an influence also; for the action of the Covenanters in 1639 and 1640 had provided an example of successful resistance to royal authority in defence of national and religious claims. It was in these circumstances that a group of Irish conspirators planned a general insurrection throughout the country, for which the signal was to be the seizure of Dublin Castle on 23 October 1641. At the last moment, the plan was betrayed; the castle was saved; and, though insurrection broke out on the appointed day, it was at first confined to the north, where the sense of grievance among the natives was strongest.

Throughout Ulster the natives rose against the colonists, massacred many thousands of them and seized upon some of the most important towns and strongholds; but the loyalists secured Londonderry, Enniskillen and Carrickfergus, with other places of less note; and they kept control over important, though ill-defined, areas in the east and in the north-west. Elsewhere, however, the Irish forces, commanded by Sir Phelim O'Neill, dominated the province. The ultimate aim of the insurgents is a matter of conjecture; but in their public declarations they constantly affirmed their loyalty to the crown – O'Neill, indeed, claimed to be acting under direct authority from Charles himself – and they justified their conduct as a necessary defence against the aggressive policy of the 'puritan faction'.

The fate of the insurrection hung upon the attitude of the Old English, and especially upon that of the Roman Catholic lords and gentry of the Pale. Some of them undoubtedly had known of the conspiracy, but in general they were not actively involved. Their grievances were less acute than those of the Ulstermen, and their traditions inclined them to support the crown and to distrust the natives. Religion certainly formed a link with the latter; but for a long time they had enjoyed a practical toleration, and if this had seemed likely to continue they might have remained loyal or at least neutral. But they, like the Ulster insurgents, were alarmed at the attitude of the Long Parliament, which was showing itself aggressively protestant in Irish as well as in English affairs; and the lords justices who had taken over the government from Strafford were strongly puritan in sympathy. Stories of the Ulster massacres, horribly exaggerated, had aroused fury in London and panic in Dublin, and in both capitals the sternest measures were called for against all recusants, irrespective of race. In the circumstances, it was natural enough for the Old English to join with the rebels, and the greater part of them did so before the end of the year. The combined forces besieged Drogheda, a general invasion of the Pale began and the rising spread to Munster.

The horror and fear aroused in England by stories of the Irish rebellion might have been expected to produce speedy forces for its suppression. But the king had to depend on parliament for supply, and parliament, half suspecting that the king was himself in some way involved with the rebel leaders, was unwilling to trust him. The troops immediately available in Ireland were put under the command of the earl of Ormond, head of the Butler family. He was a devoted royalist and there was little sympathy between him and the lords justices, who were more inclined to favour the puritan and parliamentary side in the contemporary quarrel in England. But in the first flush of disaster they were ready to turn anywhere for help, and Ormond had a good reputation as a soldier. Under his direction the safety of Dublin was secured, and he was anxious to pass at once to the offensive before the rebels had time to organize themselves and collect arms. The lords justices, jealous of his authority, and fearful of weakening the defences of the capital, refused their consent. But by the end of the year reinforcements at last began to arrive from England, and in the spring Ormond was allowed to advance on Drogheda, which he relieved in March. In the following month the protestant position in Ulster was strengthened by the arrival of Major-General Robert Monro with a Scottish force of 2500 men. Monro had learned his trade in the Thirty Years' War, his troops were inflamed by tales of Irish atrocities, and the severities practised during his first campaign in Down aroused the indignation of even such a hardened old soldier as Sir James Turner. But he won considerable military success and established an uneasy peace over a considerable part of Ulster.

The situation in Ireland was still further complicated by the outbreak of the English civil war in August 1642. For the next seven years, until the arrival of Cromwell in August 1649, the 'war of the three kingdoms' filled the country with the conflict not only of armies but of diplomatists. There was no clear-cut division of parties. The rebels, under the direction of the Roman Catholic bishops, set up a central government with its capital at Kilkenny and summoned a 'general assembly for the kingdom of Ireland', a kind of parliament representing the native and Old English interests. They also appointed a Supreme Council to carry on the war, and made provision for local government and the administration of justice. But this 'Confederation of Kilkenny', as historians have called it, though it was in arms against the government, continued to profess loyalty to the crown and supported its claims by an appeal to Magna Carta. The native Irish and the Old English who had combined in this confederation were held together mainly by their common religion, and this bond was strengthened by the just conviction that if the puritan party triumphed they would both suffer equally. But whereas the Old English were uneasy at finding themselves in rebellion and were ready to return to their allegiance without insisting on religious concessions which the king might find it dangerous to grant, the Irish, while not disowning their duty to the crown, were more submissive to clerical direction and were unwilling to accept less than the full re-establishment of the Roman Catholic church in Ireland.

Among the protestants there was the same sort of confusion. In some measure all parties were held together by fear of the rebels; but there were those who thought English rebels as dangerous to royal authority as Irish, others who distrusted the king and placed their reliance on parliament, others who cared for neither king nor parliament so long as the result turned to their own profit.

The attitude of every group was critically affected by the land question. Most of the native Irish, and especially those of Ulster, had entered upon the war with little or no landed property; and, though they did not make any formal claim for the return of confiscated estates, it is unlikely that they would have been satisfied with a peace that did not restore some at least of what they had lost in the plantations. In any case, having less to lose in the event of defeat than their Old English allies, they were willing to stand out to the end. The Old English were, for the most part, possessed of estates; success might enrich them, but failure would be the ruin of themselves and their families; and they were ready for any reasonable settlement that would secure to them what they already had. On the protestant side, though there were a few native Irish, like Lord Inchiquin, and a few Old English, like Ormond, the majority was made up of newly planted families, of government officials and of soldiers of fortune. Many of them looked forward to the defeat of the rebels as an opportunity of making money out of forfeited estates; they opposed a compromise settlement, and, provided the rebellion was suppressed, cared little whether by king or parliament. Even in England the Irish land question affected the course of politics, for parliament had raised great sums on the security of the prospective forfeitures, and the 'adventurers' who had advanced the money used their influence to push forward the policies most likely to bring them a profit.

In this confusion of religious and political and economic motives nothing could clarify the situation save decisive military success on one side or the other; but for a long time the war dragged on inconclusively. The confederates, though they had the advantage of numbers and controlled the greater part of the country, suffered from divided leadership. Owen Roe O'Neill, nephew of the great earl of Tyrone, commanded their force in Ulster, and Thomas Preston, who belonged to a noble family of the Pale, commanded in Leinster. Both had served in the Spanish Netherlands, and a mutual jealousy there engendered made hearty co-operation between them impossible. It was mainly on this account that the confederates were never able to appoint a single commander-in-chief; and each pro-

vince had its own army under its own general. The protestants also
were divided – the Scots in the north, under Monro, the royalists of
the Pale, under Ormond, those of Munster, under Inchiquin – and the
various groups gave each other little support; but they had rather
the better of it in the desultory fighting of 1642 and 1643. During
these years the protestant forces received some further help from
England and Scotland, but attention there was naturally concentrated
on the struggle between the king and parliament. The king's chief
interest in Ireland was to make a treaty with the rebels which would
release troops for service in England. Ormond laboured hard at this
and in September 1643 he concluded a 'cessation of arms', or truce,
during which negotiations for a definitive treaty could proceed. But
progress was very slow; and, in any case, Ormond could negotiate
only for the forces under his direct command. The Scots army in the
north ignored the cessation and subscribed the Solemn League and
Covenant; the Munster protestants disowned Ormond and adhered
to the English parliament, which had condemned the cessation
without waiting to hear its terms.

Ormond's difficulties were increased by the king's duplicity. As the
royal cause in England became more desperate, Charles's scruples
about concessions to the Irish recusants weakened. He opened secret
negotiations through the earl of Glamorgan, an English Roman
Catholic, who made a treaty which the king was obliged to repudiate
as soon as it became public. But the Irish and clerical party in the
confederacy, strengthened by the arrival of a papal nuncio, Rinuccini,
wished to reject Ormond's more moderate proposals and to insist
upon the confirmation of the Glamorgan treaty. For a time, however,
the Old English dominated the Supreme Council and in March 1646
a treaty was made with Ormond, though its publication was postponed. Less than three months later, and before the treaty could take
effect, came the first great battle of the war, which temporarily
altered the balance of power in the confederacy and put Rinuccini in
control. On 5 June Owen Roe O'Neill and the Ulster forces inflicted
a crippling defeat on Monro at Benburb, seven miles from Armagh.
Monro's army was not wiped out, but he lost all his artillery and a
great quantity of arms, and for a time he ceased to be dangerous. The
military results of the victory were surprisingly small, for O'Neill
failed to follow it up. The political results were more important;
O'Neill's influence in the confederation was greatly strengthened,
and with his support Rinuccini was able to overthrow the Supreme
Council, establish himself in control and secure the repudiation of

the Ormond peace. But the dissensions within the confederacy could not so easily be got rid of, and though Preston joined forces with O'Neill for an attack upon Dublin their mutual distrust brought it to nothing.

Though Dublin was saved for the time being, Ormond's position had become almost impossible. He could not hold out much longer without help, and no help could be expected from the king, who had lost his last army and was now virtually a prisoner. Help might, indeed, be obtained from the English parliament, but only in return for submission to parliament's authority. Ormond was thus in a dilemma, for he must surrender either to Irish or to English rebels. It was mainly in the hope that king and parliament might yet come to terms and save Ireland for the protestant faith and the English interest that he chose the latter course. On 18 June 1647 he handed over Dublin and the other garrisons that he still held to a parliamentary commander, and a month later sailed for England.

The complicated skein of negotiations which confused English and Scottish politics for the next two years naturally included Ireland also. When the king's cause began to revive Ormond returned in the hope of building up a royalist coalition. Inchiquin had already declared for the king; and the confederates, now thoroughly frightened by the success of the parliamentary forces, concluded a new treaty (January 1649) by which they agreed to fight for the king under Ormond's leadership. On this occasion, Rinuccini's protests were ignored; and he left Ireland in February. Owen Roe O'Neill, who still commanded a large army in the north, at first held aloof and then tried to come to terms with the parliamentary commanders on his own account. His final decision to throw in his lot with Ormond came too late to alter the course of events; and he himself died in November 1649. But by this time the whole situation had changed: in August Cromwell had landed at Dublin, with 12,000 men and a commission from parliament as lord lieutenant of Ireland.

Cromwell spent only nine months in Ireland and when he left in May 1650 the work of reconquest was still far from complete. But the vigour and cruelty of his campaigns and the ruthlessness of the settlement that he subsequently directed have left a mark and a memory that succeeding centuries have not been able to wipe out. He came to Ireland not only as a parliamentary commander pursuing the royalist enemy to his latest stronghold, but also as the avenger of blood, the minister (as he believed) of divine justice on those responsible for the cruelties which had been committed in the Ulster rising of 1641. It is this that explains not only the sack of Drogheda and of Wexford but even more the satisfaction that appears in Cromwell's reports. 'I am persuaded', he writes from Drogheda, after describing how 2000 men were put to the sword, 'that this is a righteous judgement of God upon those barbarous wretches, who have imbrued their hands in so much innocent blood.' It was in this spirit that the conquest of Ireland was continued by Ireton and Ludlow; with the capitulation of Galway in May 1652 the work was virtually completed. By this time the royalist coalition, never firmly united, was in total disarray. Ormond had joined Charles II in exile. Clanricarde, whom he left behind as deputy, was unable to control the rival factions. There was no authority that could either organize a united opposition to the parliamentary forces or negotiate a general peace. Scattered garrisons and individual commanders made what terms they could for themselves and their troops, but the kingdom as a whole lay unconditionally at the mercy of the victors.

The settlement of Ireland which followed this conquest was dictated by both political and economic motives. In 1652 the economic motive was the more urgent, for the claims against the prospective forfeitures were mounting steadily. The English parliament, under an act of 1642, had raised large sums on the security of such forfeitures; and those who had advanced the money, the 'adventurers', were now pressing their claims. The arrears of pay due to the soldiers and the debts due to the army contractors were also to be met out of the fruits of the conquest. By 1653 the total of these claims came to about three and a half million pounds. Besides all this, the government hoped that there would be a surplus for general purposes.

   The political motive behind the settlement appeared in the way in which it was carried out. By the Long Parliament's 'Act for the settlement of Ireland', passed in 1652, every Irish proprietor who had resided in Ireland at any period during the war and who could not prove his 'constant good affection to the interests of the commonwealth of England' was to forfeit a proportion of his estate. By this sweeping measure almost every Irish landlord, protestant and Roman Catholic, native Irish or Old English, royalist or confederate, was brought under condemnation. To clear the way for a thorough plantation, all the forfeiting landlords were ordered to remove into Connaught or Clare, where they were to receive an equivalent for the portion of their estates to which they were entitled. In their place came a crowd of new settlers, many of them officers in the commonwealth armies. In practice, this transportation was far less extensive than the terms of the act would suggest; and, in so far as it was enforced, it affected only the landlords and some of their more substantial tenants. The bulk of the population, tradesmen, farmers, and labourers, remained behind: it was a change of proprietors, not of population. But the effect of the confiscation was to alter decisively the balance of political power. In 1641 the majority of Irish landlords were Roman Catholics; after the Cromwellian settlement the majority were protestants, and the commonwealth government looked upon them as the best guarantee for the maintenance of English authority in Ireland. The same aggressive nationalism can be seen in the measures against the Roman Catholics, especially in the attempt to exclude them from cities and boroughs; for though there was a good deal of religious animosity, there was also a basic conviction that Roman Catholics could never be loyal to the English interest.

The long-drawn-out struggle of these years had a disastrous effect on the economic life of the country. The prosperity built up under Wentworth disappeared. Trade was almost at a standstill; land fell out of cultivation; war, famine and disease seriously reduced the population. Even when the actual fighting was over there was no immediate improvement, partly because uncertainty about owner-ship discouraged the careful development of estates. The depleted population was still further reduced by emigration: some thirty or forty thousand soldiers of the disbanded Irish armies, encouraged by the commonwealth government, took service abroad; and there was also a systematic policy of transporting 'vagrants' to the West Indies as indentured servants. Many of the new settlers, however, were able and enterprising men; and the economic recovery which was a feature of the later seventeenth century had begun before the restor-ation of Charles II.

The social changes brought about by the Cromwellian conquest and settlement were lasting. The constitutional changes were drastic but short-lived. In 1641 Ireland had a parliament of her own, shackled by Poynings' law and subject to English direction, but still able in some measure to represent and defend Irish interests. Under the commonwealth this was swept away; and Ireland, like Scotland, was given representation in a central parliament, which legislated for the whole British Isles. In the confusion that followed the death of Oliver Cromwell and the collapse of the protectorate this parlia-mentary union broke up. A convention representing the parlia-mentary constituencies, which met in Dublin in February 1660, asserted the right of Ireland to a distinct legislature, while at the same time repudiating any idea of separating Ireland from England. Such an assertion of national independence might seem to come strangely from the Cromwellian settlers who dominated the convention; but their main loyalty was to their newly won estates, and this seemed at the time the best means of safeguarding them. The same selfish interest led them to accept the restoration of monarchy. By this time it was a strong possibility, and some of the more far-seeing members of the convention were already in touch with the king. There was no explicit bargain, but Charles made it clear that he would respect the existing land settlement; thus reassured, the convention was ready to declare in his favour. It was, however, part of the royal policy that England should appear to lead the way; so the king's friends in Ireland held back, and he was not proclaimed in Dublin until 14 May, six days after his proclamation in London. But the attitude of the Irish Cromwellians had strengthened his hand during a critical period and he realized how important it was to retain their support.

From restoration to revolution

For Ireland the period between the restoration and the revolution was one of prolonged crisis. On the surface, there was some appearance of tranquillity. The country became more prosperous; revenue increased; despite local disturbances the authority of government was maintained; Ireland was more peaceful than Scotland during the covenanting wars, and calmer than England during the 'popish plot' scare. But there was no sense of security, for the twin problems of land and religion, which had received a violent solution under Cromwell, were naturally revived at the restoration. This revival brought little immediate benefit to the Roman Catholic gentry, for they recovered only a small fraction of their former estates, but they were not left without hope of doing better; while this hope remained the protestants in possession could not feel safe. The struggle between the parties came to the surface in the revolutionary war, but it had never been really abandoned during the interval.

The restoration land settlement failed because it was impossible to satisfy all the conflicting claims. The Cromwellian settlers had taken a leading part in restoring royal authority and Charles had bound himself to respect their rights. But other groups also had to be considered. There were consistent royalists who must be restored without delay. There were occasional royalists, who had found themselves fighting for the king at some stage of the complicated warfare of the previous twenty years and now hoped to recover what they had lost under the commonwealth. There were former rebels who claimed to be restored under one or other of the treaties made with the confederates. There were royalist officers claiming arrears of pay. There were those who had served Charles abroad, even if they had fought against his father at home, and who now flocked back in the hope of recovering something out of the general confusion.

The Cromwellians had the great advantage of being in possession, and powerful forces in England were financially interested in keeping them there. The agents of the Irish convention assured Charles that there was in fact enough land to satisfy everyone, and on the strength of this assurance he issued, in November 1660, a declaration promising to preserve the existing settlement and at the same time to ensure that no one deserving restoration should suffer. Ormond's comment on this sums up its unreality: 'There must be new discoveries of a new Ireland, for the old will not serve to satisfy these engagements.' However, a parliament was summoned to turn this declaration into an act. Here again the Cromwellians had an advantage, for being in possession they practically controlled the elections, and the new house of commons was almost completely in their hands. Something of its character can be seen in the fact that it was entirely protestant: though Roman Catholics were not yet excluded from membership by law, the recusant opposition of earlier parliaments had, in fact, been eliminated.

If it had had a completely free hand this parliament would simply have confirmed the existing state of affairs; but the operation of Poynings' law gave other interests some chance of being considered. The details of the settlement were worked out in England and the agents of the various parties concerned were allowed to present their claims. A compromise was finally reached in the 'act of explanation' (1665), 'explaining' the 'act of settlement' (1662) that had confirmed the royal declaration of November 1660 and had proved unworkable; it was heavily weighted in favour of the Cromwellians, but it did compel them to surrender something. They were to give up one-third of their holdings, and this land, with other lands confiscated by the commonwealth government but not distributed, was to form a sort of fund from which various claims could be met. It was far from sufficient for the purpose; and even claimants whose restoration was specifically provided for in the act of explanation were not always able to recover their estates.

In the long run, a considerable amount of land was restored to those who had held it in 1641, or to their heirs. But there was little order or justice in the restoration and court favour usually counted for more than merit. The many former proprietors who remained unsatisfied, most of them Roman Catholics, did not at once give up hope or tamely submit to their fate. Those whose means or influence enabled them to engage in politics frequented the court and sought allies for a general attack upon the whole settlement. Others, as after the Ulster plantation, remained at home and took to brigandage. Thus the restoration land system was subjected to constant attack. Landlords of the Cromwellian interest saw with alarm the favour shown by Charles II to Richard Talbot and other Roman Catholic claimants, who maintained a constant propaganda against the existing land settlement; and the prevalence of 'tories'* was a constant reminder of the possibility of another 'forty-one'. In the circumstances, few proprietors felt that their title-deeds, though guaranteed by act of parliament, were safe from all danger of being questioned.

The bulk of the old protestant landlords, whose claims went back beyond 1641, had either supported parliament and so held on to their estates under the commonwealth, or else, as consistent royalists, had recovered their losses shortly after the restoration. So the protestant interest in Ireland, both old and new, was substantially satisfied, while the Roman Catholics, or a great proportion of them, were in favour of a general upheaval. Naturally, then, protestant opinion was alarmed at the toleration with which Charles seemed determined to treat the latter. Their clergy, secular and regular, moved freely about the country; schools and convents were established; episcopal synods were held with at least the tacit approval of the government. There was, of course, no formal security in this toleration by connivance, as was shown during the 'popish plot' scare; but the general character of the period can be seen from the fact that the Irish commanders at Limerick in 1691, anxious to get the best terms they could, stipulated that 'the Roman Catholics of this kingdom shall enjoy such privileges in the exercise of their religion . . . as they did enjoy in the reign of King Charles II'.

---

*Gaelic *toiridhe*, 'a pursuer', hence 'a robber'. The English form of the word, in the sense of 'brigand' or 'outlaw', appears in the state papers at least as early as the 1650s.

The alarm aroused among protestants by this policy of toleration extended to England, where Irish affairs exercised great influence in the party politics of the period. The king, if he chose to press on with his 'Catholic design', could count on a great body of support in Ireland, not merely on religious grounds, but because the dispossessed Irish proprietors hoped that he would help them to recover their estates. For the same reason, the opposition looked jealously upon Ireland as a potential weapon in the king's hand for the overthrow of protestantism and parliamentary government in England. Some of the hottest debates in the English parliament turned upon royal policy in Ireland; and the general hatred and fear of 'Irish papists', sedulously fostered by the whigs, was an important factor in the overthrow of the Stuart monarchy.

The question of religious toleration was complicated by the clear emergence of protestant dissent. The various sects introduced into Ireland during the commonwealth period gradually disappeared after the restoration; and only the quakers survived into the eighteenth century as a distinct body. But the Scots presbyterians long established in Ulster were in a different position. After living uneasily for over thirty years within the pale of the established church, they had, in the 1640s, set up their own ecclesiastical system, and by the time of the restoration were organized throughout Ulster on the presbyterian model. Naturally enough, they opposed the re-establishment of episcopacy, and when they failed to prevent it were not inclined to submit. Under the commonwealth, many of their ministers had got possession of livings, especially in the counties of Antrim and Down, and they saw no reason why they should surrender them. The Irish bishops, however, without waiting for parliament to meet, resolved to enforce the law, and expelled all incumbents who had not been episcopally ordained: Jeremy Taylor, whose dioceses of Down and Connor and Dromore covered the chief area of presbyterian power, declared thirty-six parishes vacant in one day. But beyond this there was at first little actual persecution and the expelled ministers continued to live and work among their congregations.

The situation was changed by the outbreak of an abortive insurrection in 1663, for though this was mainly the work of Cromwellian 'fanatics' a few presbyterians were involved. Some ministers were imprisoned and others forced to leave the kingdom. But even then there was no regular or sustained effort to enforce uniformity, and in a few years things began to return to their former state; ministers came back to their congregations and meeting-houses were built to take the place of the parish churches which they had been compelled to restore. In 1672 Charles II began the payment, not very regularly maintained, of an annual grant of £600 to be distributed among the presbyterian ministers of Ulster. But this *regium donum* was not so much a mark of favour as a precautionary bribe; and until after the revolution the Irish government kept an anxious watch on the northern presbyterians and their frequent contacts with Scotland.

The firm assertion of episcopal authority against protestant dissenters was typical of the restored church of Ireland, which now entered upon a period of vigorous life. Convocation met once more, and, without waiting for the approval of parliament, adopted and enforced the English prayer book of 1662. The right of the clergy to tax themselves was recognized. Trinity College, Dublin, where most of the Irish clergy were educated, was reformed by Jeremy Taylor, as vice-chancellor. In the 1680s the complete Bible was at last published in Irish, but did less than its promoters had expected towards converting the 'popish natives'. The church still suffered from many abuses, but the standard of piety and learning was probably higher than it had been for centuries. The learning of churchmen was not narrowly confined, and clergy formed a high proportion of the membership of the Dublin Philosophical Society, the Irish equivalent of the Royal Society in England. But though the church was in some respects stronger than before the civil war it had become clearer than ever that it was not the church of the people. From the restoration onwards, religious life in Ireland flowed in the three well-marked streams of Anglicanism, Roman Catholicism and protestant dissent.

In spite of the instability produced by the half-solved problems of land and religion, the economic recovery which had begun under the commonwealth continued more rapidly after the restoration. The Irish economy was still essentially agricultural; and attempts during the restoration period to broaden it by encouraging textile manufacturers had, at the time, little success. But the surplus of agricultural production available for the market was increasing; and during the early 1660s the export of cattle, sheep and wool to England formed the most important element in Ireland's overseas trade. The importation of cheap Irish cattle suited the graziers of the west of England, but it alarmed the cattle-breeders of the area that supplied the lucrative London market; and the latter induced the English parliament to pass, in 1663 and 1666, acts that first restricted and then prohibited altogether the importation of cattle from Ireland. The effect of this legislation on the Irish economy has almost certainly been exaggerated: even before the prohibition had been imposed a drop in the price of cattle had made the English market much less attractive. Indeed, Ireland suffered more from the interruption of overseas trade during the Dutch war of 1665–7 than from the prohibition of cattle imports into England. The export of live cattle was, in fact, soon replaced by the more profitable export of salted beef, for which the principal markets were the West Indies and the North American colonies. The English navigation acts of the 1660s and 1670s, while restricting Ireland's access to the colonial market, did not affect the export of beef, and Ireland's transatlantic trade gradually expanded.

The improvement in the economy was reflected in a gradual rise in royal revenue. In the early 1660s parliament had supplemented the old hereditary revenue of the crown, which brought in only about £40,000 a year, by substantial subsidies; but its intention was to increase the hereditary revenue to a point at which it would be sufficient for all the regular expenses of government. To this end it imposed various new taxes, including a hearth tax, from which only the very poor were exempt; but the most significant change was a large increase in customs and excise duties, and the income from these would naturally rise or fall with the volume of trade. It was reckoned that the annual yield of the royal revenue, as now settled, would amount to about £200,000, which was more than the total cost of the civil and military establishments. In fact, it was some time before this figure was reached but, later on, it was greatly exceeded: by 1678 the revenue could be farmed out at £300,000 a year. There therefore should have been a considerable surplus; but there was so much mismanagement and peculation that, though the king and his friends drew large sums out of Ireland, the army was almost perpetually short of equipment and in arrears of pay.

The revenue as settled at the restoration, though badly mismanaged, was sufficient to make the crown independent of parliamentary supply. In 1666, when parliament had dealt with land and finance and other outstanding issues, it was dissolved; and Charles did not summon another. It was not until 1689, and then in very different circumstances, that the Irish parliament met again.

The military establishment was by far the most costly item in Irish government: in 1666, for example, it came to £168,000, or more than two-thirds of the estimated revenue. At that time the armed forces (excluding the militia, which was seldom called out) consisted of some 1600 horse and 5000 foot; and these figures, though they varied somewhat from time to time, were never substantially reduced. This was a large and expensive army for Ireland to keep up; but it was not merely a defence force against possible invasion, it was also a police force; the troops were distributed over the country in small garrisons and almost constantly engaged in the work of suppressing tories. They were ill-paid, often inefficient and sometimes mutinous, but it is hard to see how the administration could have been carried on without them. Though the Irish army was thus required in Ireland, the king was anxious to use it elsewhere; a standing army maintained out of hereditary revenue, and consequently free from parliamentary inquiry, was a source of strength which he was not likely to overlook. Charles was more cautious than either his father or his brother and did not propose to bring Irish troops into England. But in 1674 and again in 1679 an Irish force was prepared for service in Scotland, to help in suppressing the covenanters; and though it was never sent its readiness to act was of considerable value to the Scottish government. The Irish army also provided part of the garrison of Tangier. This was of double advantage to the king, for it not only saved English money but it enabled him to keep at home English troops whom he was very unwilling to send abroad.

Though the English parliament could not object to this use of Irish resources to serve the general interests of the monarchy, it did watch royal policy in Ireland with suspicion. The king had much more freedom of action in Irish than in English affairs, and parliament feared that he might use that freedom to build up financial and military resources with which to overthrow parliamentary government in England. These fears were not entirely groundless. There can be no doubt that Ireland was intended to play an important part in the 'Catholic design'; and during the cabal ministry great favour was shown to Irish Roman Catholics, and they were even given some reason to hope that the land settlement would be modified in their favour. All this drew a strong protest from the English house of commons, the king was compelled to follow a more cautious course, and royal policy received a fresh check in the outbreak of the 'popish plot' scare in 1678.

The political agitators who busily turned Oates's revelations to party advantage could not ignore Ireland, for, if there were a 'popish plot' at all, it was inevitable that Ireland, with its large Roman Catholic population, would be involved. They professed to uncover a conspiracy for the murder of Ormond, at that time lord lieutenant, and he was accordingly instructed to disarm the Roman Catholics, strengthen the garrisons and generally put the kingdom in a state of defence. But Ormond refused to be frightened. He took such precautions as he considered wise, and laboured hard to persuade the protestants that any sign of panic would be a great encouragement to their enemies. Under his confident guidance the country remained calm. But the policy of practical toleration was interrupted and Ireland supplied one of the most illustrious victims of the public frenzy, Archbishop Oliver Plunket of Armagh, a man of peaceful life and genuine loyalty. He was among the last to suffer for the 'plot'; and in the royalist reaction which soon followed the Irish Roman Catholics recovered their former freedom.

This royalist reaction, and the financial assistance of Louis XIV, enabled Charles to free himself from parliamentary control; and during the last years of his reign he moved steadily towards the establishment of an absolute and Roman Catholic monarchy. But before Ireland could play its full share in this plan the government there would have to be recast by the admission of Roman Catholics to both civil and military positions. Such a sweeping change could hardly be carried through while Ormond was lord lieutenant; though opposed to persecution, he was a strong churchman; and he would never be a willing instrument in a plot to overthrow the protestant constitution of the three kingdoms. Charles therefore decided to remove him, but died before his purpose was fulfilled, and Ormond remained in office long enough to proclaim James II. Almost immediately afterwards he left Ireland for the last time.

The event deserves a moment's retrospect, for Ormond was the dominant figure of restoration Ireland. He was lord lieutenant from 1661 to 1669 and again from 1677 to 1685, and even when he was out of office his influence was considerable. A man of ancient family and great estate, lord high steward of England, chancellor of the university of Oxford, the friend of Clarendon and one of the acknowledged leaders of the old cavalier party, he was, apart altogether from the lord lieutenancy, one of the greatest subjects of the crown. The source of his influence lay not only in these accidents of birth and breeding, but also in his own character. His parts were solid rather than brilliant. He was industrious and reliable, a shrewd judge of men and events, and above all he had a clear honesty of purpose, based on a strong though unostentatious piety. His removal from office was a turning point in the history of the British Isles, for it marked the first important step towards that breach in the old alliance of church and crown which was to prove fatal to James II.

The death of Charles and the departure of Ormond produced anxiety among Irish protestants; as the new sovereign's policy revealed itself this anxiety turned to consternation. The struggle that reached its climax at the Boyne and ended at Limerick ran a clear course from the accession of James II. The events of these years showed how completely religious and political divisions had become identified in Ireland. Once the fighting began, even protestants who professed loyalty to James were disarmed and imprisoned. At the same time, Anglicans and presbyterians sank their differences in face of a common danger. The former distinction between 'native Irish' and 'Old English', already weakened during the Cromwellian regime, now had little meaning; and 'Irish' and 'Roman Catholic' became almost interchangeable terms. But the Gaelic aristocracy and its traditions had gone for ever; the Irish of the revolutionary wars were led mainly by men of English descent.

James knew that Englishmen were deeply interested in the maintenance of protestant supremacy in Ireland; but he wanted the help of the Irish Catholics and it was only to be secured by giving them control of the government. The agent he chose for the purpose was one little likely to reassure protestant opinion. Colonel Richard Talbot was the brother of the Roman Catholic archbishop of Dublin; during the reign of Charles II he had engaged in various schemes for the overthrow of the restoration land settlement, and the English house of commons had urged the king to remove him from court. He was a brave man, but unreliable and something of a braggart, not greatly respected even among his own party. In 1685 James made him earl of Tyrconnell and sent him to Ireland to carry out the new policy. Within a short time the army was purged of protestants; Roman Catholics were appointed as judges and admitted to the privy council; the municipal corporations were remodelled so as to secure Roman Catholic majorities. In Tyrconnell's mind the crown of this work was to be a parliament in which the acts of settlement and explanation would be repealed and the old proprietors restored to their estates. While James remained on the English throne he was not likely to consent to a measure which would destroy one of the main guarantees of English power in Ireland; but the English revolution and James's flight to France in December 1688 altered the situation. Ireland had contributed substantially to James's over-

Modern Ireland

Coleraine
Londonderry
CO. DONEGAL
CO. ANTRIM
ULSTER
Lough Neagh
Belfast
Dungannon
Benburb
CO. DOWN
Sligo
Enniskillen
CO. MONAGHAN
Dundalk
CO. CAVAN
CONNAUGHT
Battle of the Boyne
Drogheda
Athlone
Maynooth
Dublin
Galway
LEINSTER
Wicklow
Limerick
Tipperary
Wexford
Waterford
Dingle
MUNSTER
Cork
Bandon
Kinsale

‐‐‐ Boundary of Northern Ireland
‐‐‐ Provincial boundaries
▨ Areas included in James I's plantation in Ulster

throw, for thousands of Irish protestants, alarmed at Tyrconnell's policy, had flocked over to England where they added to the general discontent and alarm; and James's calling in of Irish troops had done more than anything else to turn public opinion against him.

Events in England did not at once affect Tyrconnell's power. He continued to rule in James's name and the greater part of Ireland still acknowledged his authority. The one centre of resistance was in the north, where the protestants were strong in numbers as well as in property, and here William and Mary were proclaimed king and queen in March 1689. But the protestant forces were not well organized and after one brief encounter in the field they were glad to take refuge behind the walls of Enniskillen and Londonderry.

This was the position when James himself landed at Kinsale in March 1689. His main aim was to use Ireland as a base for the recovery of England; but he was now so completely in the hands of the Irish that the settlement of their claims could no longer be delayed. In May a parliament met in Dublin.* The measures taken by Tyrconnell against the corporations, the flight of so many protestants and the state of affairs in Ulster combined to produce a house of commons which was almost exclusively Roman Catholic and a house of lords which was predominantly so. This assembly carried through a social and political revolution with which James had little sympathy, for he was still an English king and so bound to support the English interest in Ireland. He resisted successfully a demand for the repeal of Poynings' law; but he could not prevent the passage of a 'declaratory act' denying the right of the English parliament to bind Ireland and forbidding appeals from Irish courts to the English house of lords. It was this act especially that, later on, earned for this parliament the title of the 'patriot parliament'. Other measures established formal liberty of conscience and largely disendowed the church of Ireland. But the great work of the 'patriot parliament' was the making of a new land settlement. This was accomplished by two acts. The first repealed the acts of settlement and explanation and so restored the legal situation to what it had been before the insurrection of 1641. The second was an act of attainder, of which the practical effect was to confiscate the estates of over 2000 protestant landlords. James opposed the latter, because he knew how disastrous it would be to his interests in England; but parliament forced it through and took

*This parliament was subsequently declared invalid. Apart from the question of James's legal title at the time, the procedure required by Poynings' law was not followed, for obvious reasons.

the precaution of limiting the royal right of pardon. This new land settlement, despite all that has been said against it, was neither more nor less just than the Cromwellian and restoration settlements which it reversed. Like them, it was really an act of war; and people who are struggling, or believe they are struggling, for life, land, liberty and religion usually look to the end rather than to the means, and seldom worry about nice points of legality or justice.

While the Irish parliament was thus dividing the spoil the task of securing it was going forward but slowly. In April, James marched north to restore his authority in Ulster, and after some delay concentrated his forces against Londonderry, the chief centre of resistance. The city was closely besieged for fifteen weeks, but in spite of great privation held out until the arrival of an English squadron with supplies and reinforcements obliged the besiegers to retire. The interval thus gained was of great importance to William, for it enabled him to prepare an expeditionary force in England. This reached Ulster in August 1689 and kept the way open until William himself arrived, in June 1690, with a large and efficient army. In the meantime, James had received a reinforcement of 6000 troops from France. On 1 July the two armies met on the river Boyne, some three miles above Drogheda, and James was decisively beaten. The battle was of great importance to England and France as well as to Ireland. It was a blow to Louis XIV's prestige, even though it was balanced by a French naval victory off Beachy Head the previous day. For William it meant that his position in England was now secure; and though the war in Ireland dragged on for over a year, James himself recognized the final nature of his defeat by leaving the country almost immediately. But the battle had a purely Irish as well as an international significance. The instinct that has kept its memory alive in Irish politics is a true one, for the Boyne was the critical moment of a long struggle between the Roman Catholic and protestant interests. The fact that the protestants were allied with England and led by a Dutch prince, while the Roman Catholics were allied with France and led by an English king, might complicate the situation but could not alter its essential character. The 'protestant nation' which was to dominate Ireland in the eighteenth century here established its supremacy; and Irish protestants, even when engaged in a determined struggle to free themselves from the control of the English parliament, never ceased to honour the 'glorious and immortal memory' of William III.

After the Boyne William occupied Dublin without resistance, and there the war should have ended. The Irish had given up hope of victory and fought on only for reasonable terms, which William, anxious for a quick settlement, was quite ready to grant. He proposed to offer a general guarantee of life and lands to all who submitted; but (says Bishop Burnet) 'the English in Ireland opposed this. They thought the present opportunity was not to be let go of breaking the great Irish families'. A proclamation which promised merely life and personal estate produced no effect, and the war continued until the last Irish force surrendered at Limerick in October 1691. Sarsfield, the Irish hero of the revolutionary war, had defended the city gallantly while any hope of effective aid from France remained, and in the end he was able to secure fairly good terms, embodied in the famous treaty of Limerick. The military articles of the treaty provided for the transport to the continent of those Irish soldiers who wished to take service abroad. The civil articles contained a general promise that the Roman Catholics should have the same degree of toleration as in the reign of Charles II, and there were particular stipulations for the estates and other interests of gentlemen then in arms and those under their protection. On these terms Limerick was surrendered, and thousands of Irish troops went abroad, the beginning of that 'flight of the wild geese' which was to draw off from Ireland almost all that was best among the remaining gentry of Gaelic and Old English blood. The military articles were carried out on the spot; the civil articles required parliamentary confirmation, which the king had promised to make every effort to secure. But the Irish parliament proved obstinate, William had to give way on many points, and when at length the articles were confirmed in 1697 it was in a form that conferred little advantage on those whom they were intended to benefit.

4 The Protestant nation, 1691-1800

Ireland after the revolution

The end of the revolutionary war reproduced in some measure the conditions of 1603. Another conquest had been completed and once more Ireland lay helpless before the conqueror. But behind this similarity there was an essential difference, arising from the confiscations and plantations which had taken place in the interval. In 1603 the whole of Ireland was for the first time brought under effective English control and the administrative and legislative system had to be adapted to the new circumstances; in 1691 there was an administrative and legislative system already in existence over the whole country and there was a loyal population ready to work it. Ireland had been reconquered not only for the crown but also for the 'English of Ireland'. Though these were for the most part descended from settlers of the Tudor and Stuart periods, they included also significant Old English and native Irish elements: their distinguishing mark was not their racial origin but their protestantism. The 'protestant ascendancy' thus established lasted throughout the eighteenth century and was only gradually broken down in the nineteenth.

The ascendancy was in origin and purpose a colonial garrison, politically and socially dominated by the landed class, but spread through all ranks of society. But though difference of religion prevented its absorption by the Roman Catholic majority and though it never ceased, in some ways, to be English, it rapidly developed a spirit of independence. The more secure it felt at home the more bitterly did it resent the restrictions placed by England upon its parliament and its trade, and the more strongly did it assert the national claims of Ireland. In an age when political power was so closely linked with property it was almost a matter of course that the Irish landlords should assume that they were the natural rulers of the country; and it was understandable, at least, that the protestants in general – landlords, lawyers, bankers, merchants, farmers – since they alone enjoyed full rights of citizenship, should come to think of themselves as 'the Irish people'. Though they did not forget their English heritage, they could yet claim to be the representatives of an ancient kingdom whose rights it was their duty to defend. Thus there grew up in eighteenth-century Ireland a nationalism that owed nothing to Hugh O'Neill or Patrick Sarsfield, that commemorated the battle of the Boyne and stood fast by the protestant succession, but that was determined to free Ireland from the domination of the English parliament.

In retrospect, this nationalism must appear too narrowly based to achieve permanent success: protestant domination in Ireland could hardly be maintained indefinitely without support from England; and the protestant minority must either pay the price of this support or surrender power to the Roman Catholic majority. But Irish protestants themselves saw things differently. Even in the immediate aftermath of the revolutionary war, which had demonstrated clearly enough their dependence on British arms, they found occasion to assert their right to manage affairs in their own way.

Though the confiscations that followed the war had reduced the area held by Roman Catholic landlords to about one-fifteenth of the kingdom, the protestants were still jealous of their political power and anxious to restrict them still further. They resented the tolerant spirit of William's administration. When the Irish parliament, now an exclusively protestant body, met in 1692 it showed itself so aggressive, both in asserting its own constitutional claims and in attacking the indulgence shown to Roman Catholics, that William dared not ask it to confirm the civil articles of the treaty of Limerick. A later parliament, in 1697, did confirm the articles, though in a mutilated form; but in defiance of the whole spirit of the treaty and against the king's wishes it also initiated a series of penal enactments against Roman Catholics, which, with additions from time to time, continued to be at least nominally in force until almost the end of the eighteenth century.

These penal laws have been compared with the almost contemporary French laws against the Huguenots, upon which they may have been partly based; but the circumstances in which they were enacted and the ends which they served were very different. They were directed against the religion of the great bulk of the population, not against that of a tiny minority; they arose from political fear, not from missionary zeal or an authoritarian desire for uniformity; their general purpose was degradation rather than conversion. The Irish penal code, unlike the French, cannot be regarded as religious persecution, in the strict sense of the term, for there was no effort to suppress Roman Catholic worship. An act of 1703 provided for the registration of 'popish priests', and though laws were passed for the expulsion of dignitaries and of regular clergy, they were not enforced. But while their worship was to be tolerated the Roman Catholics themselves were to be deprived of all political influence. They were excluded not only from parliament but also from the army and the militia, from every branch of the civil service, from municipal corporations and from the legal profession. They were forbidden to send their children abroad to be educated, and efforts were made to keep all education at home under the control of the established church.

All these restrictions bore most heavily upon the gentry, and it was against them that the penal code was really directed. The peasantry were not regarded as dangerous, but the few surviving Roman Catholic proprietors were. For this reason parliament was above all determined that land, the key to political power, should not pass into their hands. They were forbidden to acquire it from a protestant by purchase, inheritance or gift, nor might they lease it for a longer term than thirty-one years. A Roman Catholic proprietor had no power to leave land at will. On his death it was to be divided among his sons, but if the eldest became a protestant he was to inherit all. If his conversion took place during his father's life-time the latter became merely a life-tenant, without power to alienate any part of the estate. If a protestant woman, owning land, married a Roman Catholic her land passed at once to the protestant next-of-kin; if a Roman Catholic wife turned protestant all her real property was released from her husband's control. Thus the amount of land held by Roman Catholic proprietors could not increase and was almost bound to diminish.

The whole of this penal system was not and could not be rigidly enforced. Children were frequently sent abroad to be educated, and schools were established at home. Bishops and regular clergy moved about the country with some inconvenience, but little danger. Even the land laws could be evaded, and some Roman Catholic families retained their estates entire throughout the whole penal period, sometimes with the co-operation of friendly protestants. But in its general purpose the system was successful. The Roman Catholic majority soon ceased to be dangerous; the Jacobite insurrections of 1715 and 1745 produced no disturbance in Ireland; and until the land purchase schemes of the nineteenth century the bulk of the land remained in protestant ownership. Those of the Roman Catholic nobility and gentry who retained both their estates and their faith throughout the penal period sometimes professed to speak for the whole body of their co-religionists; but it is very doubtful how far they either understood or sympathized with the outlook of those whom they claimed to represent. Conservative by tradition, and nervous of attracting the suspicion of the government, they had no desire to arouse popular feeling. When, in the nineteenth century, Catholic nationalism became the dominant political force in Ireland, it was not to the Catholic landlords that it looked for leadership. Its essentially middle-class and clerical character can be traced, at least indirectly, to the effectiveness of the eighteenth-century penal code.

The Irish parliament was equally determined to have its own way in dealing with the protestant dissenters. It rejected William III's proposal for a toleration act, complained bitterly about the payment of *regium donum*, which he had renewed and increased, and even brought about its temporary suspension at the end of Anne's reign. In Anne's reign, also, a sacramental test was imposed. This excluded protestant dissenters, as well as Roman Catholics, from the public service and, what was of far more importance to them, from municipal corporations. Though parliament did not take the initiative in the matter, it accepted the test, and steadily resisted all the efforts of English whig governments to have it repealed.

This policy of exclusiveness was frequently condemned, both by the dissenters themselves and by their whig allies in England, as ungrateful and impolitic. The part played by the presbyterians in resisting James II, and the apparent need for uniting the whole protestant interest of Ireland against the Roman Catholic majority, might seem to give weight to this condemnation. But it is not hard to see the motives that influenced the churchmen. The presbyterians of Ulster, though they did not include many landlords, were strong in numbers and organization, and in many areas they had established a virtual monopoly of trade. They made no effort to conceal their hostility to the episcopal system and their frequent contacts with Scotland kept ever before them an example of presbyterian triumph. Bishops and landlords naturally looked with anxiety upon such a strong and hostile body, and thought more of present rivalry than of former alliance. Besides this, they were convinced, and with reason, that if any danger of Roman Catholic domination should recur the presbyterians would be bound to throw in their lot once more with the established church and, for their own sakes, support the revolution settlement to the end, even if they considered it in some respects unfair to themselves.

As the century progressed both sides became more tolerant. The effect of the sacramental test was mitigated by a series of indemnity acts, and the test itself, so far as it affected protestant dissenters, was finally removed in 1780. But by this time there was a new factor in the situation. The fear of political domination by the Roman Catholics had greatly declined, and the more liberal-minded among the presbyterians were ready to accept them as allies against the whole system of privilege on which the protestant ascendancy was built. This alliance, incomplete though it was, helped to produce the revolutionary turmoil in which the parliamentary independence of Ireland was destroyed.

The degradation of the Roman Catholics and the exclusion of the protestant dissenters from public life strengthened the political position of the church of Ireland, and during the eighteenth century it enjoyed a greater degree of security than at any period since the reformation. This did not lead to any considerable expansion. The civil power was satisfied to safeguard the church without attempting to enforce uniformity and the church itself showed little missionary zeal. Some Roman Catholics of the land-owning class conformed under pressure of the penal laws and a few presbyterians with political ambitions did the same, but the bulk of the people were unaffected. In the early part of the century the church was active in struggling for the rights of convocation and for internal reform. But the government's policy of appointing English whig bishops to the more important sees soon produced a change, and though the spirit of tory high churchmanship never quite disappeared, the church establishment came to be regarded as little more than a department of state. Indirectly, however, the church could still exercise a strong influence through parliament, as appears, for example, in its resistance to the removal of the sacramental test.

The Irish parliament was able to maintain the strictly Anglican character of the protestant ascendancy, even against the pressure of English whig governments, because it had itself acquired a new importance. In the later middle ages it had represented little more than the four 'obedient shires'. During the sixteenth century it represented a progressively wider area, but its meetings became infrequent and irregular; in Elizabeth's reign, for example, there were only three, and each was called to deal with some specific question. Wentworth's attempt to use parliament as a normal instrument of government was intended solely for the benefit of the crown, and the experiment was a short one. At the restoration, the Irish parliament had a chance of acquiring the same sort of influence as the English, for the hereditary revenue was now hopelessly insufficient to meet the cost of government. But parliament increased this revenue so generously that the king was made independent of further supply, and the opportunity was lost. By 1692, however, government expenditure had once more got ahead of income, and this time, instead of increasing the hereditary revenue again, parliament granted 'additional duties' for a limited period. In Anne's reign it became the established practice to grant these duties for two years at a time, and thenceforward parliament had to be called at least every second year. It was therefore not until after the revolution that Ireland became in fact what she had long been in theory, a parliamentary monarchy. The Irish parliament had thus little more than a century of continuous existence. The rapidity with which it built up its traditions and the degree of maturity that it attained in that brief period are far more remarkable than the corruption and bigotry which are often the only things remembered about it. During the seventeenth century it had managed, in spite of Poynings' law, to establish some degree of initiative in legislation, by the practice of introducing 'heads of bills'; and by the early eighteenth century this had become the normal procedure. These 'heads' were bills in all but form, and could be freely debated and amended. If passed, they were submitted to the lord lieutenant and council to be approved first by them, then by the king and council in England and so sent back to be laid before parliament. It was a clumsy and defective procedure. Heads of a bill might be suppressed or altered in either council. If they were suppressed parliament had no remedy; if altered, it could only accept or reject the bill in its new form.

This parliament was not, in any modern democratic sense, representative of the country, or even of the Anglican minority. There were boroughs as 'rotten' as any in England: Clonmines had only one house, Harristown had none at all, Bannow was a mountain of sea-sand. Even in boroughs which had a larger population the parliamentary franchise was often confined to a small group, under the control of a 'patron' who was usually a neighbouring landlord. The buying and selling of seats was at least as widely practised as in

England. The county elections were often genuine contests, but they were contests between landlords; for the forty-shilling freeholders, who formed the electorate, were mostly tenants and could generally be counted on to vote as their landlords directed, though sometimes – and especially in Ulster during the latter half of the century – they showed a considerable degree of independence. During the greater part of the century the representative character of parliament was further weakened by the infrequency of general elections. Until 1768 there was no statutory limitation on the life of a parliament; and it might last until it was dissolved by the demise of the crown. Thus, one parliament lasted throughout the reign of George I, another throughout the reign of George II.

In many respects the Irish parliament bore a strong resemblance to the English, but there was a fundamental difference between the constitutions of the two kingdoms. In Ireland, the executive, headed by the lord lieutenant, was imposed from outside. Parliament might accept or reject the lord lieutenant's policy but could not get rid of him, for he was the nominee of the English ministry of the day. During the first half of the eighteenth century he was normally an an absentee, coming over at two-yearly intervals to conduct a session of parliament. The visit generally lasted about six months and was almost wholly taken up in the management of the house of commons; for his great task was to form and maintain a government party which would defend him from attack and ensure that the necessary legislation, above all the supply bills, got through safely. It was impossible to calculate in advance how things would go, for party divisions were even less clearly marked and less stable than those in the British parliament at the same period; and the methods of parliamentary management sometimes employed at Westminster were absolutely indispensable in Dublin, if the authority of the British ministry over Ireland was to be maintained. There was a body of place-holders, on whom the government could usually rely, and there was a solid core of malcontents – 'the standing, sour opposition of the house', as a contemporary called them; there was an ill-defined group of 'country gentlemen' – composed mainly, though not exclusively, of county members – who usually supported the government from a sense of duty as well as from hope of reward; but the general character of the house appears most clearly in the comparison of it to a highland army, a collection of clans or groups, each gathered round a chief. The rival ambitions and shifting alliances of these groups formed the pattern of parliamentary politics.

To build up a government majority out of such discordant elements was an exhausting task and involved protracted negotiations with everyone who had or might have influence in the house. The most constant element in the situation was the selfishness of the members, whose support had generally to be secured by titles, places and pensions for themselves, and civil, military and ecclesiastical appointments for their relations. A majority so composed was apt to disintegrate, and throughout the session the lord lieutenant had an almost daily struggle to hold it together under the stress of internal rivalries and personal ambitions.

There was another, and greater, danger, against which it was difficult to guard in advance. Both in parliament and in the country there was a continuous, though fluctuating, tradition of patriotism, an 'Irish interest', as opposed to the 'English interest' of the government. Any measure which caught the popular imagination as detrimental to Ireland might lead to public demonstrations in Dublin, and a flood of protests from grand juries and corporations throughout the country. The house of commons, in spite of its unrepresentative character and the selfishness of its members, could sometimes be very sensitive to this sort of public opinion; a vigorous opposition might spring up and sweep into its ranks the bulk of the government's allies, until even the very place-men, whose duty it was to support the lord lieutenant through thick and thin, would hesitate to stand out against the popular will. But an opposition of this sort had even less cohesion than the mercenary majority of the government. The lord lieutenant had only to wait for the excitement to subside, reconstruct his party and go on as before: the Irish house of commons might, on occasion, defeat the policy of the ministry, but could not drive it from office.

Economic and social conditions

During the eighteenth century Ireland enjoyed a longer period of internal peace than ever before. There were local agrarian disturbances, which sometimes reached serious proportions; but between the end of the revolutionary war and the insurrection of 1798 there was no general threat to the existing order. The economic and social benefits of this long-continued peace were very unequally distributed among different sections of the population; but there can be no doubt that the country as a whole was much better off at the end of the period than at the beginning.

This improvement was not continuous, nor was it equally marked in all areas. After the treaty of Limerick the economy quickly recovered from the disruption caused by more than two years of civil war; and during the 1690s Ireland was relatively prosperous. But this prosperity did not last; and the early decades of the eighteenth century were a period of widespread depression. The change has commonly been attributed to the restrictions placed on Irish trade by the English parliament, and especially to an act of 1699 which prohibited the export of Irish woollens to any country except England, from which they were already virtually excluded by heavy duties. But the effect of these restrictions has been exaggerated. The woollen industry was still on a small scale: in 1698 woollen goods accounted for only ten per cent of the value of Irish exports. Besides this, the circumstances that made its products competitive in the European market – in particular, the relatively low cost of manufacture – were changing, so that further expansion of the export trade was, at best, problematical. The reason for the depressed state of the country during the first half of the eighteenth century lay elsewhere.

The economy depended predominantly on the export of agricultural products: it was the lack of a steady market for these products, and the low prices generally prevailing, that lay behind the widespread poverty so evident during the first four or five decades of the century. Farmers could rarely accumulate enough capital to tide them over bad seasons; and a succession of crop failures, with a consequent rise in the price of food, could result in famine conditions, as happened in the south-west in 1727–9 and over a wider area in 1740–1. The situation may have been made worse by the fact that such a high proportion of land was given up to pasture. But grain prices were generally low; landlords and tenants alike found pasture more profitable; and legislation designed to encourage tillage had little effect. The depressed state of Ireland during this period has done much to create the gloomy picture generally accepted as characteristic of the whole eighteenth century, not least because its poverty, its dirt and its apparent hopelessness have been so vividly portrayed, not without some exaggeration, in the writings of Swift.

It was hardly surprising that Irishmen should attribute the impoverished condition of their country to the effect of restrictive English legislation and especially to the woollen act of 1699. In this way economic and constitutional issues were linked together; and in time it came to be the popular belief that Ireland could never prosper until the claim of the Irish parliament to be the sole body competent to make laws for Ireland had been recognized. Those who supported this claim were naturally inclined to emphasize the ill-effects of English legislation; and it is significant that complaints about the woollen act were much stronger in the 1720s, when the constitutional issue was acute, than they had been in 1699, when the act was passed. But even though the practical effect of this act and other measures of the same sort (e.g. the prohibition on the export of glassware, imposed in 1746) have certainly been exaggerated, it is likely that they tended to discourage enterprise. An Irish industrialist might well hesitate to put capital into a manufacture that might, if prosperous, be deprived of any outlet overseas by an act passed at Westminster. The rapid industrial expansion in the 1780s and 1790s, after the British parliament had surrendered its claim to legislate for Ireland, would certainly suggest that this latent threat had had an inhibiting effect.

In all circumstances, however, the economy was bound to depend mainly on agriculture; and the character of Irish life was largely determined by the structure of rural society. In Ireland, as over most of western Europe, by far the greater part of the land was held by landlords and worked by their tenants. The landlords, as a class, were neither so tyrannical nor so careless as tradition has painted them; but, generally speaking, they did less to develop their estates and improve the condition of their tenants than landlords in England. There were, of course, numerous exceptions. Many landlords were involved in the establishment and running of the Dublin Society (now the Royal Dublin Society), founded in 1731, which had among its objects the improvement of agriculture, and which was one of the first and most successful undertakings of its kind in Europe. Especially among the great proprietors, who had estates or interests in England as well as in Ireland, there was a high proportion of absentees; and the fact that much of their Irish income was spent outside Ireland was a loss to the economy. But an absentee landlord was not necessarily a bad landlord: the Abercorn estates in Ulster and the Shelbourne estates in Munster were among the best managed in the country. It was, in fact, among the resident landlords, and particularly among those of small means, that one was most likely to find examples of the tyranny commonly associated with the landlord class as a whole.

The landlord's control over his tenants was, however, most commonly limited by the terms of a lease; for in the eighteenth century the majority of Irish tenants were leaseholders, with secure possession for the period specified in the lease. By an act of 1704 Roman Catholics could not hold leases of longer than thirty-one years; but with a protestant tenant it was in the landlord's interest to grant a lease for lives,* for such a lease made the tenant a free-holder, with a right to vote in parliamentary elections; and a land-lord's political influence depended very much on the number of votes he could influence. A lease for lives put the tenant in a very secure position; and even a lease for thirty-one years was not unlikely to outlast the life of the person to whom it was granted. In economic terms, a great deal naturally depended on fluctuations in agricultural prices. The rent remained fixed throughout the duration of the lease: if prices fell, the tenant's margin of profit fell with them; if they rose, it increased. The growing prosperity that distinguished the second half of the century from the first was largely due to a fairly steady rise in the price of agricultural produce. Though there were bad seasons and crop failures from time to time, no disaster comparable with the famine of 1740–1 occurred again until the nineteenth century.

Leaseholding tenants formed, under the landlords, the top layer of the agrarian community; they were reasonably secure and many of them were well off. But other sections of the population were much less comfortable. Some leaseholders (commonly called 'middlemen') sub-let the whole or part of their holdings, naturally exacting from the sub-tenants a substantially higher rent than they themselves paid. Worse off still was the large body of labourers. Some of them lived with the farmers for whom they worked; others were allowed to occupy a small plot of ground on which they could build a cabin and grow food for themselves and their families, the rent being set off against their wages. These 'cottiers' (as they were called) formed the poorest and most vulnerable section of rural society, for labour was plentiful, so that wages remained low and employment was uncertain.

The position of the cottiers almost certainly got worse as popula-tion grew. The rate of growth is a matter of some doubt; but it seems likely that in 1700 the population stood at around 2,500,000, that it rose to around 3,000,000 by the middle of the century and to between

---

*A lease for lives remained in force so long as any one of a number of persons, usually three, specified in the lease, was alive. If, as sometimes happened, the lessor and one of his sons were included among the three lives the family might retain possession for two generations.

4,500,000 and 5,000,000 at the end. An agrarian economy cannot easily absorb such an increase; and it was the cottiers who suffered most. It was they, for example, who first came to depend heavily on a potato diet, though even at the end of the century total dependence on the potato was still unusual.

The cottiers formed only one element in the rural population; but in accounts of the eighteenth-century Irish countryside written by travellers from England or the continent the cottiers often occupy such a prominent place that one might be led to believe that they formed almost the whole of it. And in other respects, too, such accounts can be misleading. Travellers were often making, consciously or unconsciously, a comparison between England and Ireland; and in comparison with England, one of the most highly developed and prosperous countries in Europe, Ireland must have seemed poor and backward. But in comparison with conditions prevailing in some parts of the continent – in rural Norway, for example – the lot of the Irish cottier would have seemed much less wretched.

The difference between the Irish and English situations was not, however, simply a matter of economic development. In England, landlord and tenant generally shared a common religious tradition, with all that that implied, and they had a sense of security bred by generations of peaceful and orderly government. In Ireland, the landlords were almost all protestants, while most of their tenants, except in the province of Ulster, were Roman Catholics. The memory of war, conquest and confiscation still survived. Over much of the country the everyday language of the peasantry was still Gaelic; and Gaelic songs, poems and traditional tales kept alive a sense of cultural distinctiveness. There is plenty of evidence to show that this state of affairs did not preclude the possibility of friendly relations between landlord and tenant; but it did provide conditions in which disputes, if they arose, might easily become violent and enduring.

Though the state of Ireland in the aftermath of the revolutionary war, and especially during the depression and poverty that marked the early part of the eighteenth century, might seem likely to breed agrarian interest, the country remained peaceful. It was not, indeed, until the latter half of the century, when economic recovery was already well advanced, that organized violence appears; and it was not, in origin at least, a campaign of tenants against landlords. Its beginning can be traced to a specific cause. Much of the best land in Munster was farmed by tenants with very large holdings, on which they raised cattle for the export trade; and when, in 1759, the removal of English restrictions on the import of cattle and beef from Ireland offered them a new market, these graziers enclosed large areas of common land in order to extend their pastures. These enclosures provoked a violent reaction, organized by the 'Whiteboys', so called because of the white smocks they wore on their nocturnal forays. The Whiteboys, once established, soon extended their activities. They attacked tithe-collectors, for tithe has always been an unpopular charge, even where (as in England and France) it was paid to the church of the majority, and even more so in Ireland, where it was paid to the church of a small minority. They sought to impose on the Roman Catholic clergy a scale of charges for their services. They tried to insist on the right of a tenant to have his lease renewed when it expired; and if, instead, the farm was transferred to someone else, the new tenant was likely to be attacked.

Some contemporaries believed that the Whiteboy movement was political in purpose and fomented by French agents. But there is no foundation for this belief, which may have arisen from the fact that there was frequent clandestine intercourse between Ireland and France: it was in France that a large proportion of the Roman Catholic clergy received their education; and some recruiting still went on for Irish regiments in the French service. The fear of French intrigue may have helped to account for the severity of the acts passed against the Whiteboy movement; but, despite all the efforts of government, it continued; and the tradition of agrarian violence, once established, survived into the next century.

The Whiteboy movement spread from Munster into parts of Leinster; but until the 1790s, when political and sectarian issues gave rise to conflict, the rest of the country remained peaceful, apart from two brief outbreaks in Ulster. In 1763 mid Ulster was disturbed by the 'Oakboys', who protested against the administration of an act that required tenants to assist in the making of roads and against what they regarded as an over-strict exaction of tithe. Almost ten years later, the action of a County Antrim landlord, Lord Donegall, in demanding such heavy payments on the renewal of leases that many farmers had to give up their holdings, provoked violent retaliation by the 'Steelboys' (or 'Hearts of Steel') who attacked the new tenants and their property. Both these outbreaks were stimulated by local and temporary grievances; and the organizations disappeared when the immediate cause of their formation had passed.

These violent interludes are not at all characteristic of eighteenth-century Ulster, which was not only generally peaceful but also, in comparison with the rest of the country, prosperous. This state of affairs may have been partly due to the stronger sense of community between landlords and tenants; but it probably owed more to the presence of a flourishing linen industry.

Linen had been woven in Ireland from early times; but it was only in the eighteenth century that it became an important national industry. The government did a good deal to encourage it. Irish linen was given preference in the British market and the Irish parliament voted large sums to promote its manufacture. The importance of this financial support must not, however, be exaggerated. Most of it went to Leinster and Munster, where the industry never became firmly established, and comparatively little to Ulster, which soon became its main seat. It is not easy to explain why this should have been so; but the development certainly owed something to the energy and enterprise of a group of English immigrants who built up a small but prosperous linen manufacture in County Armagh in the later seventeenth century. It was probably the existence of this manufacture that attracted to the north French protestant refugees driven from their homes by the policy of Louis XIV; and their skill and experience contributed to its later expansion.

The Ulster linen industry was organized on a domestic basis; and its beneficial effect was felt throughout the province. But it benefited other parts of the country also: much of the yarn used by Ulster weavers was spun in Connaught; and for a long time the bulk of the export trade went through Dublin. Spinners, weavers, bleachers, carriers, merchants and bankers all derived profit from the manufacture and marketing of linen, which was, after agricultural produce, by far the most important item in the national economy. Thus, the industry was, directly or indirectly, of advantage to the whole country; but it was in the north that its benefits were most apparent.

Ulster, despite this comparative prosperity, was the only part of Ireland from which there was substantial emigration during the eighteenth century. It had begun around 1717, at a time when the economy was still depressed; the existence of a fairly substantial transatlantic trade meant that transport was available; and once the example had been set, the process continued, even when the economic situation became better, until it was interrupted by the outbreak of the American war in 1775. The emigrants were, for the most part, presbyterians of Scottish extraction, who resented the privileged position of the established church; they left home with a sense of grievance, and their influence helped to push the colonists along the path to complete independence.

The unaccustomed peace of the eighteenth century has left an enduring memorial in its architecture. To this period belong the most distinguished of the country houses, large and small, which are to be found in every part of Ireland and which were designed for comfort or for show rather than for defence. Not only peace but economic growth as well had a beneficial effect on the towns; and the eighteenth century is the great period of Irish urban architecture. It is the public buildings, the stately mansions and the residential squares of the eighteenth century that still lend distinction to Dublin; and the general drabness of many a country town is relieved by buildings of the same period.

The expansion of urban life reflected the growth in numbers and influence of a middle class, made up for the most part of professional men, bankers and merchants. In the circumstances of the time it was natural that a high proportion of this middle class should belong to the established church; but in the province of Ulster it contained a great many presbyterians and, especially in the latter half of the century, the Roman Catholic element steadily increased. It is hardly surprising, then, that it was members of this class who took the lead in attempting to break down the denominational barriers by which Irishmen had been so long and so sharply divided.

But this attempt belongs to the closing decades of the century; and it proved almost wholly abortive. For the great bulk of the population difference in religious faith, and above all the difference between protestant and Roman Catholic, remained more important than difference in rank or wealth. Among protestants, indeed, the effect of class distinction was modified by a considerable degree of social mobility; and luck or talent might raise a man from humble beginnings to a position of affluence and even of power. This, in turn, strengthened the basic sense of community natural to a self-conscious minority: even the poorest protestant could feel that he had, or might have, some share in the 'ascendancy' that protestants as a whole enjoyed in the life of Ireland. This sense of a common interest was to be of essential importance to the leaders of the ascendancy in their effort to establish the legislative independence of their country.

The winning of a constitution

The discontent of the protestant ascendancy naturally found expression in parliament, which in spite of all its defects as a representative assembly could always provide a platform for the assertion of Irish rights. From the revolution onwards it had struggled intermittently to establish two claims: the first was its own sole right to legislate for Ireland; the second, the principle that supply bills should not be drawn up in England and presented ready-made, but should take their rise in the form of 'heads' in the Irish house of commons. The former claim was laid down by William Molyneux in his *Case of Ireland's being bound by acts of parliament in England, stated,* published in Dublin in 1698 – a book which the English commons immediately condemned for its 'bold and pernicious assertions' of Ireland's legislative independence. But the claim still remained, and in George I's reign the English parliament tried to quash it finally by a declaratory act asserting its own authority 'to make laws and statutes of sufficient force and validity to bind the kingdom and people of Ireland'. (This statute is generally known, from the regnal year in which it was passed, as 'the sixth of George I'. It also took away the appellate jurisdiction of the Irish house of lords.) The question of the supply bills also became a matter of serious dispute during the 1690s and the struggle continued, in various forms, for the next sixty or seventy years.

Though the lord lieutenant could generally, by means already indicated, secure a majority in the house of commons, the task was always more difficult when these or other matters affecting the constitution or welfare of Ireland were at issue, for on such occasions the Irish interest would receive many recruits in the house and much noisy support in the country. The inconvenience which this might cause the government was demonstrated in the prolonged struggle over 'Wood's halfpence' which lasted from 1723 to 1725. Ireland was short of copper coinage, and authority to coin halfpence and farthings was granted to William Wood of Wolverhampton. There was an immediate outcry in Ireland against the manner in which the grant was made, against the quality of the coins and against the quantity to be issued. Public feeling, once aroused, could not be kept within the limits of the original dispute. Swift, in his *Drapier's letters*, raised the whole question of Anglo-Irish relationships, and indignantly denied that 'the people of Ireland are in some sort of slavery or dependence different from those of England'. This dangerous excitement was shared by the Irish parliament. In the house of commons the government could not find a single member to oppose the demand for an inquiry into the grant, and even the most docile office-holders would do no more than attempt to tone down the addresses against it which both lords and commons presented to the king. In the end the government had to give way; the lord lieutenant was recalled and another sent over in his place to announce that Wood's authority had been revoked. The constitutional agitation, deprived of its immediate stimulus, now died as quickly as it had arisen. But the government did not ignore the lesson of its defeat; and during the next decade a more efficient way of managing the house of commons was gradually worked out. The direct responsibility of the lord lieutenant for building up and maintaining a government party declined; and the task was left to two or three of the leading members of parliament. These 'undertakers' guaranteed to put through government business, especially the granting of supplies, and in return they were entrusted with a considerable share of crown patronage. This method of management, often called the 'undertaker system', restricted the authority and lowered the prestige of the lord lieutenant, but it assured him a quiet session during his six months' visit to Ireland.

The undertakers were entrusted with the management of parliament for the specific purpose of securing the passage of government measures, but they soon developed a distinct interest of their own, based on their parliamentary influence. 'The lord lieutenant', says Charlemont, 'was wholly in their power, and could confer no favour but at their recommendation.'* Any attempt on his part to rely upon other advisers would produce the threat of a dangerous revolt. In some respects the situation resembled that in the early Tudor period, when government was left in the hands of an Anglo-Irish noble who maintained royal authority in return for a considerable degree of independence. In the sixteenth century the only alternative to the rule of Kildare was the appointment of a strong English chief governor, backed up by an English army; in the eighteenth century the only alternative to the undertakers was a resident lord lieutenant backed up by the full authority of the British government. But this alternative would have required a strong and consistent Irish policy such as no British government of the period was capable of producing.

*James Caulfeild, first earl of Charlemont, was the political ally of Flood and Grattan, and commander-in-chief of the volunteers (see pages 111-12).

Something of the character of Irish political life at this time can be seen in the course of a parliamentary dispute of the 1750s. The Irish parliament claimed the right to dispose of surplus revenue. The British government denied this and insisted that it was a royal prerogative. The excitement, both in parliament and in the country, was as great as that aroused over Wood's patent, and in some respects it was more dangerous, for the undertakers themselves turned against the lord lieutenant, espoused the popular cause and brought about the defeat of the government in the house of commons. But though this dispute showed how easily patriotic, or at least anti-English, feelings could be aroused among the Irish gentry and the Dublin mob, its conclusion showed also how completely the country was lacking in constructive leadership. The undertakers had appealed to these feelings almost entirely for selfish ends. They felt their monopoly of influence threatened by the political machinations of the primate, George Stone, and were anxious to convince the lord lieutenant that they were indispensable to the peaceful conduct of affairs. In this they were at least partially successful. The most important of them, Henry Boyle, speaker of the house of commons, was bought off with an earldom and a pension, and his chief colleagues were similarly satisfied. The deserted patriots had no alternative leaders to turn to, and were obliged to vent their feelings in execrations; the mob, which had once escorted Boyle in triumph from the parliament to his house, now, with equal enthusiasm, burnt him in effigy.

The disappointment of the mob was justified, but the constitutional questions which had been raised were not entirely lost sight of. In the words of Lord Charlemont, Irishmen 'were taught that Ireland had, or ought to have, a constitution'. Within ten years the lesson had been learnt and under more efficient and honester leaders the Irish interest began to acquire some of the cohesion of a patriot party. Charles Lucas, the 'Wilkes of Ireland', after a long career of agitation against abuses in public life, entered parliament for the city of Dublin in 1761. Henry Flood, a much younger and abler man, entered in 1759. The immediate objects for which they and their allies struggled were security of tenure for the judges, the passage of a habeas corpus act, the establishment of a national militia and the limitation of the life of parliament.

This desire to share in constitutional privileges long enjoyed in England was typical of the patriots' outlook. Though determined to establish the rights of Ireland they had no thought of separation.

Like the Catholic confederates of the 1640s they regarded Ireland
and England as sister kingdoms, held together by loyalty to the same
crown and entitled to the same liberties. 'Am I a free man in England',
asked Swift, 'and do I become a slave in six hours by crossing the
channel?' But they claimed these liberties, in the first place, for the
protestant population. Many of their leaders were strongly opposed
to the claims of the Roman Catholics; and even those who favoured
their admission to political privileges were determined, at the same
time, to maintain a protestant ascendancy. 'I love the Roman
Catholic', said Grattan, in response to an address from the corporation of Dublin, 'I am a friend to his liberty, but it is only inasmuch
as his liberty is entirely consistent with your ascendancy, and an
addition to the strength and freedom of the protestant community.'

The ultimate success of the patriots resulted, in part at least, from
a change in British policy towards Ireland. Early in the reign of
George III the British government decided to break the independent
power of the undertakers by appointing a resident lord lieutenant
who would have effective control of the administration. There was
some delay in making this policy effective; but Lord Townshend,
who was sent over in 1767, remained continuously in Ireland until
1772; and by that time he had carried through his task. Thenceforward the lord lieutenant himself was the great dispenser of
patronage and the active manager of the house of commons. The
patriots gained one immediate advantage from Townshend's policy.
Partly to gain popularity, partly to undermine the influence of the
undertakers, he had supported the demand for a limitation of the
life of parliament, an octennial act had been passed in 1768, and the
patriots naturally benefited from the resulting increase of popular
influence in the house of commons. But the final suppression of the
undertakers produced a far more significant result. The lord lieutenant was now brought directly into the political conflict, and as
the representative not only of the king but also of the British government he was the symbol of that dependence of Ireland upon England
which the patriots so strongly resented. The government found it
increasingly difficult to play off one Irish party against another and
was eventually forced into a decisive trial of strength, in which all the
discontented elements in the country were ranged on the patriot side.

Townshend's victory over the undertakers came at a time when
the difficulties of Irish government were increasing. Heavy expenditure during the Seven Years' War had raised the national debt to an
unprecedented figure, and this not only provided a target for popular

criticism, but made it more important than ever to secure regular and substantial parliamentary supplies. The dispute with the American colonists made things worse. Irishmen were naturally interested in a country with whose population they had such close family ties, and they could not help recognizing that the constitutional question was directly relevant to their own situation. As a Dublin newspaper expressed it: 'By the same authority which the British parliament assumes to tax America, it may also and with equal justice presume to tax Ireland without the consent or concurrence of the Irish parliament.' It was, however, some time before the patriots were able to turn the situation to advantage. Even in 1775, after war had actually begun, Flood accepted the post of vice-treasurer, convinced that the policy of opposition was a barren one and that he could gain more for the country in office. But the patriots continued their policy under the leadership of Henry Grattan, who entered parliament in the same year and whose eloquence at once raised him to a position of great influence.

Circumstances were now working in the opposition's favour. The dislocation of trade and the rise in prices produced by the war resulted in bankruptcies, distress and unemployment. The patriots at once attributed these evils to a government embargo on the export of provisions, though in fact the provision trade (which supplied the armed forces) was more flourishing than ever. The truth or falsehood of the patriot propaganda mattered little, the important thing was that it aroused bitter resentment against England, concentrated public attention on commercial restrictions and led to an almost universal demand for 'free trade'. In this way Ireland's constitutional claims were closely associated with material grievances and a vigorous public opinion was maintained. A strong government might still have controlled the situation. But Buckinghamshire, the lord lieutenant, though by no means the 'fluttered imbecile' which Froude called him, was not a strong man in a crisis, and Lord North, almost overwhelmed with domestic and foreign difficulties, gave him very uncertain backing. The entry of France into the war and the consequent threat of invasion revealed the full helplessness of government in Ireland. Most of the troops had been withdrawn; though a militia act had been passed, there was no money to put it into force; privateers were swarming around the coasts and even communications with England were unsafe. It was clear that if the French did come the people of Ireland would have to depend upon themselves, and out of this state of affairs sprang the volunteer movement.

The first **regular** company was formed in Belfast early in 1778; by the end of the year this example had been followed over the whole kingdom, and so, instead of a militia under government control, there came into existence a national volunteer army. The volunteers were exclusively protestant. For the most part they were merchants, tradesmen and well-to-do farmers, officered by the nobility and gentry; to use Grattan's phrase, they represented 'the armed property of the nation'. The government could neither disband nor control them. They were responsible to no authority save that of their own councils and conventions, but they professed great respect for the Irish parliament; and they soon provided the patriot opposition with what it had hitherto lacked, a national organization that could arouse and maintain popular support for its programme in every part of the country.

The French invasion did not come, and it may have been partly because they were not called on for active service that the volunteers turned so readily to politics. From the first they had taken a particular interest in the trade question. Their uniforms were all of Irish cloth. Their councils passed resolutions and drank toasts in favour of 'a free trade for Ireland'. In the autumn of 1779, when parliament met, they gave more forcible expression to these sentiments. While the house of commons demanded free trade and voted supplies for six months only, the volunteers held a great parade in Dublin (significantly, it was to commemorate the birthday of the protestant hero, William III) and decorated their brass cannon with the threatening placard 'Free trade – or else'. Such an onslaught, combined with the almost desperate condition of British arms in America and of tory politics at home, forced Lord North to make concessions, and acts were passed through the British parliament removing most of the restrictions on Irish trade.

The victory was great, but insecure and even dangerous. It was based partly on the temporary weakness of the British government and partly on the support of the volunteers. But the government might recover, and the same authority which had removed the restrictions might reimpose them. The volunteers had been easy to arouse, but would it be possible to control them? For the time being it was the former question which engaged the attention of the patriots. Lord North had spoken of the trade concessions as 'resumable', and it was urged in Ireland that the only way to guarantee their permanence was to establish the exclusive right of the Irish parliament to legislate for Ireland. But a resolution to this effect, moved in the commons by Grattan in 1780, was indefinitely adjourned; for the house, though strongly affected by public opinion, was not yet prepared to defy the government openly. In the following year attempts to secure the modification of Poynings' law failed also, though Flood, now once more in opposition, supported them. From these parliamentary defeats the patriot leaders turned to the volunteers. In February 1782 a convention of delegates from the volunteer corps of Ulster met at Dungannon and passed a series of political resolutions drawn up by Grattan, Flood and Charlemont. The most important were those which asserted the sole right of the Irish parliament to legislate for Ireland and declared that the powers exercised by the privy councils of the two kingdoms under Poynings' law were 'unconstitutional and a grievance'.

The armed force behind this declaration made it formidable, but its speedy fulfilment was due quite as much to a change of government in Great Britain. In March 1782 Lord North resigned and was succeeded by a whig ministry under Rockingham. Though the whigs were sympathetic towards the Irish claims and though some of the new ministers were in friendly touch with the patriot leaders, it is doubtful how much of the Dungannon programme they would have conceded if they had been given time for negotiation. But Ireland was in a state of expectancy which would not tolerate delay. Before the whigs had been a month in office, and when the new lord lieutenant whom they sent over had been barely two days in Dublin, the Irish parliament met, and an address to the king, which was virtually a declaration of independence, was moved in the house of commons by Grattan and carried unanimously.

Whatever hesitation the government may have felt before, it now yielded completely, and within a brief space the British and Irish parliaments passed a series of acts which placed the constitutional relations between the two kingdoms on a new footing. The British parliament, by repealing the 'sixth of George I', virtually gave up its claim to legislate for Ireland. An act of the Irish parliament (usually known as 'Yelverton's act') drastically modified Poynings' law. In future, the lord lieutenant and council in Ireland were to transmit to England, without alteration, all measures submitted to them by the Irish parliament, and no others. But the powers of the king and council in England were not entirely taken away; though they were not to alter or add to a bill they might suppress it altogether, but, in practice, this power of suppressing bills was allowed to lapse. Other measures provided for the independence of the Irish courts and for the security of tenure of the judges. All these measures taken together form what is often called 'the constitution of 1782'. But it was neither, like the British constitution, a matter of long growth, nor, like the American, a coherent system set out in a single instrument. The rights which it secured to the Irish parliament were greater in theory than in practice and its weaknesses were fully revealed during the eighteen years of its existence.

Grattan's parliament and the legislative union

The years between 1782 and 1800 are generally referred to as the period of 'Grattan's parliament', and, though many other people contributed to the establishment of parliamentary independence, there is justice in the title. Grattan represented much of what was best in the Anglo-Irish tradition, though he was not entirely free from its characteristic faults. It was he who had led the patriot opposition during the difficult years that preceded the formation of the volunteers; it was he who had brought the force of volunteer opinion to bear upon the government; it was he who had carried through the parliamentary campaign that had led to success; and it was he who had launched parliament on its new career of liberty in one of his most famous speeches:

I found Ireland on her knees, I watched over her with an eternal solicitude; I have traced her progress from injuries to arms, and from arms to liberty. . . . Ireland is now a nation. In that new character I hail her, and bowing to her august presence I say, *Esto perpetua!*

With the opening of the new era there came a quickening of economic development. The removal of trade restrictions in 1779 had not brought much immediate benefit, but the effect was increasingly felt during the next few years. The woollen industry revived rapidly, though it failed to develop a large export trade. Cotton, encouraged by parliamentary bounties and protected by a heavy tariff, expanded so greatly that it came to rival linen. Other existing industries developed and new ones were established. Not unnaturally, parliamentary independence came to be associated in the public mind with national prosperity; and it is certainly true that parliament did try to encourage trade and industry, and especially agriculture, upon which the prosperity of Ireland must always in the long run depend. An act of 1784 ('Foster's corn law') did a great deal to increase the area under tillage. By a system of bounties it encouraged the growth of corn, and more and more land was brought under cultivation. In another way, also, the country drew economic advantage from the establishment of parliamentary independence, for the increased prestige of the Irish parliament led many former absentees to spend more of their time and money in Ireland, and especially in Dublin, which now reached the height of its fame and splendour as a capital. The country towns also felt something of the same influence, and one traveller after another remarks on the widespread signs of increasing prosperity.

The benefits of this prosperity went, for the most part, to the middle and upper classes. Manufacturers, merchants and bankers profited from the expansion of the economy and the rise in exports; and landlords were able, on the expiry of leases, to raise rents. But the advantageous effects of economic expansion were felt even beyond these groups. For the lease-holding tenant a continuing rise in agricultural prices offset any rise in rent; and for the labouring classes generally, it was very important, especially in a period when population was rising, that there was some expansion of employment, both in town and country: the extension of tillage, for example, meant that much more labour was required on the land.

Despite all improvement, however, the root causes of economic and social discontent remained and could still give rise to violence, as, for example, in Munster, where there was a revival of Whiteboy activity in the 1780s. Though such activity had no political content, the sense of grievance from which it sprang was later to be used for political ends by leaders who drew their inspiration from the example of revolutionary France. At the time, however, this development could hardly have been foreseen; and the potential threat was unrecognized. It was on constitutional rather than social issues that attention was concentrated both in parliament and in the country.

Though the constitutional changes of 1782 had been greeted with enthusiasm, the situation they created was not a stable one. There was no firm basis of agreement among Irish politicians. Many had been swept reluctantly along by the rising tide of nationalist fervour, and had supported the cause of parliamentary independence merely because they saw the hopelessness of opposition and wished to be on the winning side. Even among the victorious patriots there were deep differences of opinion. This was natural enough, but the personal ambition of Flood made the situation dangerous. Since his return to opposition in 1779 he had struggled hard to recover his former leadership, and to this end had constantly pressed his demands beyond the limits proposed by Grattan. He refused to be satisfied with the concessions made by the British government in 1782 and asserted that the new-found liberty of the Irish parliament was not secure, that the repeal of the 'sixth of George I' was not enough, that if the British parliament had had the right to legislate for Ireland before that act was passed the right was not affected by simple repeal. He therefore demanded that the British parliament should also renounce explicitly any claim to bind Ireland. Flood's argument may have had some legal justification, but it was impolitic to press victory to its utmost limits; and though he had his way, the 'renunciation act' which the British parliament passed in 1783 added nothing to the real security of Irish freedom.

There was more serious and more lasting difference among the patriots on the question of parliamentary reform. Here again Flood went beyond Grattan both in end and method. Grattan had expressed the hope that the volunteers, their work accomplished, would leave parliament to use the freedom they had won for it; Flood, on the other hand, was foremost among those who urged them to continue their political activities until parliament itself had been reformed. In 1783 he asked permission of the house of commons to bring in a reform bill which had the support of a volunteer convention then assembled in Dublin. But the house was not disposed to share its authority and refused permission, on the ground that to grant it would be to submit to external pressure. There was sound reason in this, but natural selfishness had at least as much to do with the decision; placemen and borough-owners had no desire for parliamentary reform. This rebuff, and their own internal disagreements, rapidly weakened the political influence of the volunteers, and the demand for parliamentary reform fell temporarily into the background.

The discussion of parliamentary reform inevitably brought forward the question of admitting Roman Catholics to political power, and the deep differences which were immediately revealed indicate one of the fundamental weaknesses of the constitution of 1782 – its failure to solve the problem of the relations between the protestant ascendancy and the Roman Catholic majority. It was essentially a constitution for the protestant nation. The penal laws, which had been less and less strictly enforced as the century progressed, had been greatly relaxed by relief acts in 1778 and 1782; but the political disabilities on Roman Catholics remained: they could neither sit in parliament nor vote at parliamentary elections. These restrictions were becoming more difficult to maintain. There was an increasing body of protestant opinion in favour of their removal; and among the Roman Catholics themselves the nobility and gentry who had survived the penal period and, even more, the growing middle class had begun to take an active interest in politics. Though they had not been allowed to join the volunteers, many of them had given financial support to the movement and had rejoiced at its success. The volunteers in general had supported the removal of restrictions on Roman Catholic worship and education; but on the question of political rights they were divided. Flood opposed concession, Grattan supported it; but the latter repeatedly expressed his devotion to the maintenance of a protestant ascendancy, and indeed, as long as parliament continued to represent the landed property of the country there was little danger of its ceasing to be predominantly protestant. The division of opinion on this question among the volunteers was one reason for the decline of their political influence. But the question itself remained active, and the growing dissatisfaction among the Roman Catholics proved very useful to political agitators of a different stamp.

The failure to solve the problem of Roman Catholic claims was not the only weakness of the constitution of 1782. It failed also in its primary purpose of settling Anglo-Irish relations on a permanently satisfactory basis. The nature of the difficulties to be overcome was imperfectly realized at the time. Neither Grattan nor Flood seems to have understood the importance of the distinction between legislature and executive. They concentrated on securing the legislative independence of the Irish parliament, but they were apparently content to leave government in the hands of an executive over which that parliament had only an indirect and imperfect control. After 1782, as before, Ireland was ruled by a lord lieutenant who exercised very much the same sort of power as a prime minister in England, and who was virtually appointed by and responsible to the British cabinet. He continued to maintain control of parliament by the same means as before; and for the general purposes of administration he could generally count on a safe majority. But there were dangerous possibilities in the existence of two formally independent legislatures in a single monarchy. In 1785 their mutual jealousy helped to prevent the conclusion of an Anglo-Irish commercial treaty which would have been to the advantage of both countries. In 1789, when George

III became for a time too ill to govern, the Irish parliament insisted upon recognizing the Prince of Wales as regent of Ireland, before the English parliament had taken corresponding action, and only the king's recovery prevented a constitutional crisis.

In spite of these weaknesses and dangers the constitutional experiment of 1782 might have succeeded but for the French revolution. For Ireland the effects of this were fatal. All the elements of unrest were encouraged, and it became more and more difficult to maintain the authority of government. The outbreak of war made things worse, for now there was the danger of French invasion to be faced. To the British government Ireland was the weak point in the line of defence, and the task of securing it was made more difficult by the existence of an independent parliament whose claim to represent the Irish people was being constantly and violently challenged. These were among the principal factors which led to the legislative union.

In Ireland as in England the outbreak of the French revolution produced a wave of enthusiasm among the supporters of reform, particularly among the presbyterians of the north, where the ground had been prepared by the influence of American ideas. In Belfast the fall of the Bastille was celebrated along with the battle of the Boyne, and throughout the country the cause of parliamentary reform was vigorously revived. But the reformers now included a strong body who could not be satisfied by the removal of the most glaring abuses of the existing system; they called for a total sweeping away of the constitution and the construction, from first principles, of an ideal democratic state. These changes were most vigorously urged by the societies of United Irishmen, founded at Belfast and Dublin in 1791, partly under the inspiration of Wolfe Tone, a young Dublin barrister, who had been carried away by the religious and political principles of revolutionary France. Though the United Irish movement was protestant in its origins, rationalist in its leadership and radically democratic in its aims, it derived much of its political importance from its alliance with Roman Catholic leaders, whose claim to political rights it strongly supported.

This union of hostile forces naturally alarmed parliament and it was quite ready to support the government in repressive measures. On the question of concessions to Roman Catholics the position was more complicated. Left to itself, the Irish administration would have met their claims with unbending resistance; but Pitt hoped to buy their support, and under strong pressure from England an act restoring to them the parliamentary franchise was carried in 1793. This marks a turning point, for it forced the protestant ascendancy on to the defensive. The right of Roman Catholics to exercise political power had been recognized, and there was no longer any logical ground for excluding them from parliament. Even as it was, a reform of the parliamentary system would now give them a great, and perhaps irresistible, influence in the government of the country. The outbreak of war with France in the same year ended whatever chance there was of a peaceful compromise. The opponents of reform were strengthened in their determination to resist any further concessions; while among the reformers there was now a growing party that not only looked to French example but hoped for French help in overthrowing the existing regime by force.

The struggle which arose out of these circumstances and disturbed the last decade of the century was not one between Ireland and England, but one between the Irish parliament, representing the property of the kingdom, and a group of radical reformers who wished to make it representative of the whole population and who, to gain their ends, were prepared to use violence at home and to ally themselves with the king's enemies abroad. There was still a liberal parliamentary opposition, led by Grattan, which continued its demand for reform and urged the need to conciliate the Roman Catholics by further concessions. But this opposition was out of touch with reality: its remedies took no account of the changed situation brought about by the French revolution, and its most far-reaching concessions would have done little to placate men bent on a complete reconstruction of the state. For an attempt to suppress the United Irishmen had driven the society underground and had brought the extremists into full control of the movement. The most immediate threat to the government came from Ulster. It was here that the United Irishmen were strongest, here that republican ideas borrowed from America and France had taken deepest root, here that men were genuinely filled with a humane enthusiasm which overflowed distinctions of creed and class. But throughout Ireland as a whole there were comparatively few who responded to such leadership, and even in Ulster they were a minority. The economic depression which came with the war stimulated agrarian unrest, always endemic in Ireland, and in the north this took a sectarian character which not only divided Roman Catholics from protestants, but churchmen from dissenters. The aggressively protestant Orange societies, which sprang up about 1795, were composed almost exclusively of churchmen and professed a strong loyalty to the crown and constitution; they supplied many recruits to the yeomanry corps raised at this time for the maintenance of order. By 1797 Ireland, and especially Ulster, was in a state of submerged civil war in which political and sectarian differences mutually inflamed one another. The grip which the Irish government had on the situation was a precarious one and it was certain that, if any considerable French force should land, a dangerous and possibly disastrous rebellion would break out.

By this time the leaders of the United Irishmen were determined on violent action and were only awaiting a suitable opportunity. At first they relied upon help from France. But a French expedition of 1796 failed; and after the British naval victory of Camperdown it was hopeless to expect a large invading force. So they resolved to strike without further delay and to trust to their own strength. The whole country had suffered severely under the system of military rule by which the Irish government had tried to crush the revolutionary spirit, and the United Irishmen hoped that the indignation, fear and hatred thus aroused would give vigour to a rebellion. The secret of the conspiracy was ill-kept, the government knew of all that went on, and on the eve of the date fixed for the rising the most important of the leaders were arrested. Lord Edward FitzGerald, an aristocrat turned rebel, brave, enthusiastic, over-sanguine, died from wounds received while resisting arrest. Wolfe Tone himself was in France* and only local leaders were available to take charge. The rising broke out on 24 May 1798; six weeks later only a few hunted fugitives remained in arms.

The rebellion was practically confined to the counties of Antrim, Down and Wexford, though there were minor skirmishes in Wicklow and north Leinster. In Antrim and Down some thousands of United Irishmen, mostly presbyterian farmers, turned out with pike and musket; but there was no backbone in the rising and three slight engagements sufficed to scatter them decisively. The fighting in Wexford was much more severe. There, the principles of the United Irishmen and the French revolution counted for little; the driving forces were religion and resentment at military rule. The peasantry, armed for the most part with pikes and led by their priests, seized

---

*In 1798, after the rebellion was over, Tone returned to Ireland with an unsuccessful French expedition. He was captured, and committed suicide in prison.

the town of Wexford and got control of most of the country. But they had no plan of action, the people of the neighbouring counties did not follow their example, and there was nothing for them to do but hold out as long as possible against the ever-increasing forces which the government brought against them. The courage of their resistance was only equalled by the ferocity with which they too often avenged their grievances on those whom they made prisoner.

The significance of the insurrection, brief though it had been, can hardly be overestimated. It established a tradition of revolutionary violence which, from that time onwards, has exercised an influence, varying in strength but never negligible, on Irish politics; and this tradition still contains all those incongruous elements that were at work in 1798 – national feeling, radical democracy, social discontent, religious fanaticism and humanitarian philosophy. In its immediate effects also the rebellion was of crucial importance. It had thoroughly alarmed not only the government but the whole protestant ascendancy. They seemed caught between the old power of Rome, reviving and militant, on the one hand, and the new danger of radical democracy on the other. The fear which this double threat aroused goes far to explain the cruelty with which the Wexford rising was crushed and leads on directly to the passing of the act of union.

The idea of legislative union had, from time to time, been considered by statesmen on both sides of the channel; but it was the insurrection that convinced Pitt of its necessity. In 1798 both administrations set themselves to prepare the way for it. The main resistance was naturally in the Irish house of commons. Personal interest, national pride, a sense of public duty, all combined to arouse opposition to such a measure. Cornwallis, the lord lieutenant, Castlereagh, the chief secretary, and Lord Clare,* who had long been one of the leading members of the administration, threw all their energies into winning a majority, and their efforts were backed by bribery more extensive than any yet known in the Irish parliament. A substantial opposition remained to the end, but though its members voted solidly together against the union, they were not agreed on any positive policy. Some, led by Grattan, were ready to make wide concessions to the Roman Catholics; others wished to maintain the existing position. Few of them seem to have faced the fact that the maintenance of the government's authority now depended directly

*John Fitzgibbon, first earl of Clare; attorney-general, 1783; lord chancellor, 1789.

upon military aid from Britain. If Britain demanded legislative union as a condition of that aid it was useless for them to refuse, unless the refusal were accompanied by some other feasible plan for securing the protestant church and the British connection, to both of which they professed their devotion; but they had no such plan to offer. Outside parliament the resistance to union was badly organized and, in general, unenthusiastic. Fears arising out of the state of Ireland and the state of Europe, and the hopes which the Roman Catholics had of getting better terms from a British than from an Irish parliament combined to produce a general inertia. It was the barristers, the Orange societies, and the church of Ireland, all associated with privilege and ascendancy, that provided the backbone of the national resistance.

From the British point of view the union was little short of a military necessity. The second coalition was breaking up and Britain was once more alone in the struggle with France. A restless Ireland was a source of intolerable danger. Ireland conciliated and closely bound to Britain would be a source of strength, especially to the armed forces, for at this time Ireland contained approximately one quarter of the total population of the British Isles. Indeed, Pitt's main purpose in seeking a union was to open the way for a policy of conciliation that the Irish parliament, left to itself, was unlikely to follow; and he let it be known that in his opinion union should be accompanied by the admission of Roman Catholics to membership of parliament, a policy generally known as 'Catholic emancipation'. The Roman Catholic bishops and landlords, encouraged by this hope, were almost unanimously in favour of union, though their clergy and people gave them little active support, and seem to have been, for the most part, indifferent. But Pitt's first task was to get the union through the Irish house of commons, where a promise of emancipation was not likely to ease its progress; and, though he certainly intended that emancipation should follow, he carefully avoided any formal commitment. To many Irish landlords, indeed, including Lord Clare, the strongest argument in favour of the union was the belief that by no means could the protestant ascendancy be saved. They accepted it in this spirit, and the act soon came to be regarded as a bulwark of protestantism.

The two identical acts which brought the separate existence of the Irish parliament to an end passed through the parliaments of both kingdoms in 1800 and came into force on 1 January 1801. Henceforth

Great Britain and Ireland were to be merged into one 'United Kingdom' with one parliament. In this new parliament Ireland was to be represented by four spiritual and twenty-eight temporal lords in the upper house, and by one hundred members in the lower. (In 1832 the numbers of Irish members in the house of commons was increased to 105.) There was to be free trade between the two countries, with certain temporary protective duties in favour of Irish goods. The exchequers and national debts were to remain distinct until they could be merged on certain specified terms, which were intended to be just to both sides; this merger did not take place until 1817. The English and Irish churches were to form the 'United Church of England and Ireland', and the maintenance of the ecclesiastical establishment in the two countries was to be 'an essential and fundamental part of the union'. On 2 August 1800 the Irish parliament sat for the last time; on 22 January 1801 the Irish lords and commons took their seats in the first parliament of the United Kingdom of Great Britain and Ireland.

5 Ireland under the union

The nature of the union

The legislative union of Great Britain and Ireland might have been a great measure; but it was conceived in a spirit of expediency and carried through by methods that seriously prejudiced its chance of success. Though it achieved the immediate purpose of strengthening Britain in the struggle against Napoleon, it was in almost every other respect a failure; and it is very doubtful if failure would have been averted even had Pitt and Castlereagh been able to fulfil their intention of securing an immediate grant of emancipation. The union was meant to solve finally the problem of Anglo-Irish relations by merging the two kingdoms in one; but in fact this never happened: Ireland retained a separate executive, and over a wide field of legislation was treated as a distinct unit. It was meant to prepare the way for peaceful government; instead, the country had to be ruled under a succession of coercion acts that were intended to strengthen the executive, e.g. by a temporary suspension of habeas corpus. The problem of maintaining law and order was never solved while the union lasted. It was meant to safeguard the protestant ascendancy; but the British government refused to be bound by the terms of the act of 1800 and having sacrificed the church in the hope of saving the landlords, then bought out the landlords in the hope of saving the union. This was a vain policy, which destroyed the power of a protestant ascendancy, bound by every tie to the British connection, only to replace it by a Roman Catholic democracy strongly inclined to seek complete independence.

The basic failure of the act of union appears in the continued existence of a separate Irish executive. The legislature had been removed to Westminster, but the lord lieutenant, the council and the law courts remained in Dublin, and the 'Castle' continued to be the real centre of Irish government. In the long run, of course, this government was responsible to parliament, and changes in party fortune at Westminster produced corresponding changes in Dublin;

but for more than thirty years after 1800 the spirit of the Irish administration remained essentially that of the pre-union ascendancy and while the union lasted the ascendancy influence was never wholly eradicated. It might be argued that the maintenance of a separate executive was a necessary part of the implied bargain by which the Irish landlord class had surrendered its control over the legislature in return for a guarantee of the protestant ascendancy, which, we must in fairness add, it identified with law and order and the rights of property. Since Ireland was to be governed in the interests of a minority the Irish executive must be on a different footing from the English. But though this executive was almost universally regarded as an instrument of the protestant ascendancy, it was also a constant reminder of Ireland's former independence. For this reason it was valued even by many of those who hated its policy: O'Connell, though he was strongly critical of almost every Irish government of his time, opposed any suggestion that the office of lord lieutenant should be abolished.

The existence of this system of Irish government helps to account for the inconsistent attitude of British statesmen towards Irish affairs. They regarded Ireland sometimes as an integral part of the kingdom and sometimes as a dependency. They could speak, for example, of '*our* duty to Ireland', thus distinguishing in their minds between Great Britain as one entity and Ireland as another. But the suggestion that this mental distinction should be turned into a legislative one shocked them. In order to understand the history of nineteenth-century Ireland it is necessary to take this paradox into full account. It arose from a factor in the situation which is sometimes overlooked and sometimes misrepresented – English nationalism. For the British statesman, and for the British public, the union of 1800 had completed a natural process by which a single system of government was extended over the whole British Isles. Regional distinction had for all practical political purposes disappeared and there was one British nation. This nation had the English monarchy and parliamentary system for its centre, English was its official and almost universal language, English wealth the main basis of its power. It was not surprising that the Englishman should come to regard the terms 'British' and 'English' as almost interchangeable. It was natural also that he should regard any attempt to break up this national unity not as a legitimate desire for self-government, such as he was prepared to approve in South America or Greece or Belgium, but as treason against the nation.

The uncertainty of British statesmen's attitude towards Ireland was intensified by their ignorance of the country. It was not ignorance of matters of fact, for the government was indefatigable in collecting information and publishing reports on almost every aspect of life – agriculture, fisheries, manufactures, population, health, education, bogs, railways, canals; it was ignorance of the country itself, of the people and their ways of thought. Gladstone, for example, despite his long interest in Irish affairs, visited Ireland only once and stayed less than a month. This ignorance, which was widespread among the British ruling class, undoubtedly strengthened the tendency to regard Ireland as a half-alien dependency. Even so scrupulous a politician as Acton sat in parliament for an Irish pocket borough without showing any sense of obligation either towards his constituents or towards Ireland as a whole.

The incompleteness of the constitutional union between the two countries was perhaps a symptom rather than a cause of Ireland's political unhealthiness. It was less obvious, but in some ways more important, that the economic union was also incomplete, in spite of the amalgamation in 1817 of the financial systems and the removal in 1825 of the temporary protection given to Irish manufacturers against British competition. Ireland was brought into the richest community in the world, but she had little share in the surplus capital of Great Britain. Some contemporaries blamed the disturbed state of the country for the fact that British industrialists showed little inclination to invest money in Ireland; but they invested freely in the republics of Central and South America, where the security was certainly no greater. Economically, Ireland had to suffer many of the disadvantages of being linked with a wealthy partner without enjoying the corresponding benefits. Lack of capital affected almost every aspect of social and economic life and had inevitable repercussions on the political situation.

This was not, however, immediately apparent. For a considerable time after the union the economic expansion that had marked the later part of the eighteenth century continued. Exports rose, in value if not in volume; and there was a good deal of capital investment. But the end of the war, in 1815, was followed almost at once by a widespread depression. The market for agricultural products shrank and prices slumped. It can hardly be said that this depression was a result of the union, for it affected other countries as well as Ireland. But elsewhere the period of depression was followed by a resumption and quickening of economic expansion, while in Ireland the rate of expansion remained low and, except in the north, manufactures made little headway. To some extent, at least, this state of affairs can be seen as an effect of the union. The economic policies followed by British governments were increasingly determined by the needs of a highly industrialized society; and Ireland (along with some areas in Great Britain) suffered in consequence.

During the first half of the century the economic weakness resulting from lack of capital was accentuated by a very rapid growth of population. From around 5,000,000 at the time of the union it rose to almost 7,000,000 in 1821 and to over 8,000,000 in 1841. This was a dangerously rapid increase in a country where the bulk of the population must depend upon the land for a livelihood; and the danger was the greater because the increase was most marked among the labouring classes and among those small-holders, especially in the west, who could hardly survive unless they could supplement the produce of their holdings by wages. The *Quarterly Review* was certainly right when it declared, in January 1832, 'The curse of Ireland is the general want of employment for its inhabitants.' And to create employment, capital was essential. The same diagnosis came from other sources also. In 1836 a committee appointed by Lord Grey to consider means of relieving poverty in Ireland recommended a scheme of public works; a few years later a royal commission on railways recommended a national system and pointed out the benefit to the whole community of the additional employment thus to be provided. But both reports were passed over. The English poor law system was extended to Ireland in 1838; and the development of Irish railways was left, for the time being, to private enterprise. The government was willing to finance road-building and similar undertakings, as a temporary measure in times of special hardship; but it rejected any general responsibility for creating employment. Its outlook, and that of the British ruling class in general, was clearly expressed in the argument of the *Edinburgh Review* (October 1837), that if the capitalists of the country could not provide work it was impracticable for the state to attempt to do so. In this and other respects Ireland suffered from the application of *laissez-faire* principles, which, however successful they might be in Britain, were ill-suited to the circumstances in Ireland.

British mishandling of Irish affairs arose largely from ignorance and neglect. But even for the best-intentioned of statesmen the task of dealing justly with Ireland was infinitely complicated by the inter-mixture of economic and political problems. The landlords represented not only a social class but a political system – the continuing protestant ascendancy. They had accepted the union, reluctantly, as the only means of safeguarding their privileged position and they were determined to maintain it to the same end. The whole local administration of the country was in their hands. They controlled the magistracy, the police, the grand juries and the municipal corporations. The removal of political disabilities on Roman Catholics in 1829 only partly altered this state of affairs; even the reform of the municipal corporations in 1840 did not bring their control to an end, and it seemed almost impossible to govern without their co-operation. The policy of the ascendancy party was to claim a monopoly of 'loyalty' and to identify agrarian outrages with acts of rebellion. But the disorder of which they complained, and which made normal methods of government unworkable, had its roots in the economic situation. On the face of it, the landlords could make out a good case for strong government support; all they wanted to do was to enforce the law, protect the rights of property and keep the country quiet. In response to every fresh disturbance they demanded, and usually obtained, sterner measures of repression; for more than twenty years after the union Ireland was governed under a series of coercion acts which suspended the normal safeguards of individual liberty. But such a system could not bring permanent peace while there was so much poverty and while the law seemed designed to protect the well-to-do. Relations between landlord and tenant were not so universally bad as has often been supposed; and tithe was resented less because of its amount than because of the way in which it was levied and, above all, because it was paid to what most people regarded as an alien church. The root cause of Ireland's distress did not lie either in excessive rents or in the imposition of tithe; but these were the grievances that touched the peasantry most closely; and both were regarded as results of a protestant ascendancy. No policy which ignored them would satisfy the mass of the people; any attempt to interfere with them would arouse the opposition of the church and the landlords and of their powerful allies in England.

The landlords were not alone in their support of the union and their demand for strong government. They had the backing of almost the whole protestant population. It was natural enough that the established church, however suspicious of the union to begin with, should speedily accept a settlement which seemed to guarantee its position, but the attitude of the Ulster presbyterians calls for some comment. They did not immediately or unanimously abandon the liberal and nationalist outlook which had characterized them at the end of the eighteenth century; and for twenty years after the union the government remained suspicious of their loyalty, though perhaps without much cause. But fear of the Roman Catholics combined with the rapidly increasing economic prosperity of the north-eastern counties to convince them that their welfare was bound up with the maintenance of the union. Relations between landlord and tenant were already much better in Ulster than elsewhere, and even the long-standing jealousy between the presbyterians and the church of Ireland was gradually broken down by the fear of a common enemy, a fear which was decisively stimulated by the new nationalism expounded by Daniel O'Connell (see pages 133–6). The dominant industrial position later attained by the Belfast area made this conversion of Ulster to the cause of union one of the most significant events in modern Irish history.

The legislative union was established in the interests of Great Britain and in some ways served those interests well; but its failure to bring about a genuine incorporation of the two countries had a profound and almost disastrous effect on British political life. Irish problems remained distinct; but now they had to be thrashed out in the imperial parliament, where they often exercised a decisive influence and consumed a disproportionate amount of parliamentary time. The growth of a strong Irish party upset the political balance: relations between the two great British parties were embittered, and a disruptive element was introduced within the parties themselves. From the time of Parnell onwards the situation became increasingly dangerous; and on the eve of the First World War the very survival of the parliamentary system in Britain seemed to be under threat.

The new nationalism

The aristocratic nationalism of the volunteers and the revolutionary nationalism of the United Irishmen were both in rapid decay at the time of the union. A sentimental regret for the glories of the Irish parliament lingered for a while among the ascendancy class, and the United Irish spirit left a brief postscript in Robert Emmet's abortive insurrection of 1803. But for many years after the union Ireland as a whole was politically stagnant. The secret societies that existed in many parts of the country – Whitefeet, Blackfeet, Shanavests,

Rockites – were not engaged in a national struggle, but in local class warfare against the landlords and against the tithe-proctors who acted for the clergy of the established church. There was all the material for a powerful political movement, but to begin with there was neither a great cause nor a great leader to unite all the various groups and inspire them with the enthusiasm of a common effort. It was the work of Daniel O'Connell to bring about this union, and in doing so he linked the cause of Irish nationalism and the cause of the Roman Catholic church so firmly together that succeeding generations have hardly been able to prise them apart.

Such a linking-up was perhaps the only means of providing the feeling of solidarity without which an Irish popular movement could hardly have emerged. There was no general sentiment against the union. The grievances of the peasantry were strongly felt and sometimes savagely avenged, but the organization of a land war on a national scale would have required a degree of co-operation and leadership which the peasantry could not supply for themselves and which, in the intellectual atmosphere of the early nineteenth century, they were not likely to get from any other class. The one issue round which it might be possible to build up a strong party was the demand for 'Catholic emancipation', i.e. the removal of the remaining political restrictions on Roman Catholics, and especially those excluding them from membership of parliament. Pitt had hoped to carry this through immediately after the union, but the opposition was stronger than he had expected, the measure had to be dropped and he resigned in protest. The Irish Roman Catholics were bitterly disappointed, but it was some time before the political possibilities of this disappointment were fully exploited. Their case was organized for the most part by noblemen and gentry who had a great respect for constitutional authority and a great fear of revolution. They had the support of many members of parliament, both English and Irish, among whom Grattan was perhaps their most faithful advocate. But even Grattan believed that emancipation was quite consistent with the maintenance of the protestant ascendancy and that the influence of property would always outweigh the influence of numbers. With such leaders and such allies the Roman Catholics were prepared to follow the most moderate methods and accept the most moderate concessions.

The advent of O'Connell changed the whole situation. He was a brilliantly successful barrister, who specialized in criminal cases; and apart altogether from his political activities he had won fame and popularity among the mass of the people, who were inclined to regard every successful defence as a victory over the government. As a young man O'Connell had used such influence as he possessed in opposition to the union and he never ceased to condemn it. At least as early as 1811 he had given public support to the proposal for its repeal; but repeal was not yet a practicable policy, and so he threw himself into the struggle for emancipation with the determination that it should lead to a popular victory, won for and by the masses. With this end in view he strongly opposed a compromise settlement, discussed between 1813 and 1815, by which the government would have been given a veto in episcopal appointments in return for the admission of Roman Catholics to parliament. Though this proposal had the support of the Vatican, it was absolutely rejected by the Irish Roman Catholic bishops, largely under O'Connell's influence.

There can be no doubt that O'Connell acted on a true instinct. A church that was even suspected of being the agent of the British government could never have become the main unifying influence in the new nation he was trying to create. But the veto question divided the ranks of those who supported emancipation and undoubtedly delayed their success. This very delay, however, left the way open for O'Connell to establish unrivalled supremacy in the movement. After a period of sporadic and fruitless effort the Catholic Association had been founded in 1823 to press the case more actively; and though it included a number of peers and other landlords it was predominantly a popular body. The parish was its unit of organization and its local agents were the parish priests. It was they who collected the 'Catholic rent', a subscription of a penny a month which provided the association with its campaigning fund, and their political influence over their people soon came to outweigh even the traditional supremacy of the landlord. The Catholic Association was the instrument by which O'Connell established and maintained his control of the movement. He had been chiefly responsible for calling the clergy into the struggle and he could count on their support. The immense resources of the 'Catholic rent' were at his absolute disposal. Against the mounting pressure of O'Connell's agitation in Ireland the British government offered a very uncertain front. Though Peel and Wellington had come into office in 1828 pledged to resist the Roman Catholic demands, their position in the house of commons was precarious, and it was by no means certain that they would be able to secure support for the additional coercive measures that would be necessary if emancipation were longer withheld. In these circumstances they decided to give way, and in 1829 parliament was opened to Roman Catholics.

The methods by which O'Connell achieved his success were no less significant than the success itself. Before his time the Roman Catholic movement was a middle-class one, under aristocratic leadership. He changed its whole character by bringing in the clergy and the peasantry. By his system of organization, by his persistent propaganda, above all, perhaps, by the great public meetings which gave full opportunity to his unrivalled powers of oratory, he used the cause of emancipation to inspire the Roman Catholic masses with a sense of united purpose such as they had never known before. He was a pioneer in bringing the force of public opinion to bear on government in a constitutional and yet aggressive way; his achievement attracted a great deal of attention outside Ireland and his example was followed both in Britain and on the continent.

Though O'Connell had promised that his campaign for emancipation would be followed by a similar campaign for repeal of the union, he allowed a decade to elapse before he took up the cause of repeal seriously. He now had a seat in parliament, where he was able to build up a party of his own from among the Irish members; and he was content, for the time being, to use the influence this gave him in order to secure reforms in the administration of Ireland. Naturally, he had most to hope from the whigs; and it was his support that enabled Melbourne to take office in 1835. Though the whigs were well disposed towards Ireland, they were themselves divided on the best policy to follow. The division was deepest on the church question, which was, after emancipation had been granted, the most controversial in Irish politics. The English and Irish churches had been united by the act of 1800 and their security had been guaranteed afresh in the emancipation act. But the union was no more than nominal, public opinion in general regarded the Irish establishment as resting on a very different basis from the English, and the defence of the former was not, as Irish churchmen had expected, made part and parcel of the defence of the latter. The line of attack that O'Connell now pressed most strongly was one with which many English whigs were inclined to sympathize. He denounced the tithe system as not only oppressive in itself, but as especially hateful to the Roman Catholic peasantry, who were compelled to contribute to the upkeep of a church which they regarded as alien and heretical. It was an old dispute, which became particularly bitter in the 1830s;

and, though O'Connell himself lent no countenance to violence, great parts of the country were convulsed by a 'tithe war', and many of the established clergy were reduced to poverty by the impossibility of collecting their dues. The whigs were prepared to alter the methods of assessment and collection so as to ease the burden on the tenantry, but they were held back from more drastic action by their own respect for the rights of property and the peers' respect for the rights of the church. So the tithe charge remained, in a somewhat modified form, and the revenue from it was not, as O'Connell and some of the English whigs desired, diverted to secular purposes. As a further concession to critics of the established church ten bishoprics were suppressed and their property applied to other ecclesiastical purposes. But though this strong assertion of parliamentary authority may be regarded as a step towards disestablishment, it was not in itself likely to conciliate Roman Catholic opinion.

This half-hearted attack on the church question was characteristic of the whigs' policy in Ireland. Urged on by O'Connell to more radical reforms, restrained by the cautious among themselves, exposed to constant attack by an aggressive opposition in the commons and hampered by the steady resistance of the house of lords, they moved from expedient to expedient, without any fixed purpose beyond the evasion of the immediate problem. But, in spite of their fumbling, they did accomplish something. They set up a national system of elementary education, they extended the new English poor law to Ireland and they reformed the municipal corporations. The wisdom of these measures may be disputed, but all of them were significant. The national schools failed to realize their original purpose of bringing together children of different religious denominations, but they raised the standard of literacy, and their influence, together with that of O'Connell and the Roman Catholic church, went far towards destroying Irish as a spoken language. The new poor law was almost entirely unsuited to Irish conditions, but it was at least a line of defence against absolute starvation. The reform of the municipal corporations was a first step towards transferring control of local government to the Roman Catholic majority. Against the whigs' failure to produce a consistent Irish policy must be set the fact that they made a notable, though temporary, change in the administration. Between 1835 and 1840 the ascendancy spirit had to give way to the liberalism of the under-secretary, Thomas Drummond. Stipendiary magistrates were appointed in large numbers to balance the influence of the landlords. Orange processions were forbidden, the control of the police was brought more firmly into the hands of the government and a larger proportion of public appointments was given to Roman Catholics.

The whole tendency of Drummond's policy was to bring more and more power into the hands of government officials and to undermine the influence of the protestant gentry. With this O'Connell was well enough satisfied, especially as his opinion was given great weight in the making of appointments; but in general he was disappointed with the results of the whig alliance, and in 1840 he prepared to bring it to an end. He was strongly influenced in this direction by the fact that Melbourne's government was obviously on the point of collapse. Peel's turn was about to come at last, and with Peel he could have no sort of understanding. Instead, he founded the Repeal Association in 1840 and renewed the policy of agitation with all the old vigour. O'Connell has been strongly criticized for his conduct at this point. He has been accused of reviving repeal in order to bolster up his declining influence in the country, or even for the sake of financial advantage. It is certainly true that his power was much less than it had been at the height of the struggle for emancipation, and that the 'tribute' (a levy which had taken the place of the 'Catholic rent' and which supplied him with his political funds) had seriously declined. It is true also that O'Connell was fond of the exercise of power, and so carelessly extravagant in his expenditure as to be continuously short of money. But, though the revival of the repeal agitation might in this way suit his own purposes, his devotion to the cause was genuine, and the political circumstances provide a perfectly adequate explanation of his conduct. There are, however, two more valid grounds of criticism. In the first place, O'Connell concentrated on constitutional and not on social issues. This was perhaps the natural result of his training and his environment, but a greater man might have seen that in the Ireland of the 1840s a purely political programme could accomplish little. Secondly, even on the political level he showed a lack of insight. In 1829 Peel and Wellington had yielded to his demand for emancipation not merely because of the state of Ireland, but because of the division of opinion in Britain. In the 1840s British opinion was solidly in favour of maintaining the union, Peel's parliamentary majority was secure, and he could safely take such measures as he thought necessary to maintain order in Ireland. O'Connell hoped to frighten him by 'peaceful, legal and constitutional' agitation. He had not considered what would happen if the agitation failed.

The repeal agitation thus launched upon its new career was intended by O'Connell to be a national movement. But, despite his pro-
testations and his efforts, its supporters were almost exclusively
Roman Catholics. He had hoped to win over the presbyterians of
the north, but in this he miscalculated almost as seriously as in his
estimate of Peel's power of resistance. His own policy of close alliance
with and dependence upon the Roman Catholic clergy had alarmed
and alienated almost the last remnants of presbyterian nationalism;
though he came to Belfast, it was to address a meeting of his co-
religionists. The spirit now dominant among the presbyterians found
its strongest expression in the speeches of one of their ministers,
Henry Cooke, an orator not altogether unworthy of comparison
with O'Connell himself, and in power of invective perhaps even his
equal. Under Cooke's guidance the presbyterians definitely ranged
themselves beside the established church in defence of the union.
There were indeed many protestants who joined the Repeal Association, and some who played an important part in it, but they were
not representative of any considerable body of protestant opinion.
Modern Irish nationalism, in so far as it springs from O'Connell, is
distinctively, almost essentially, Roman Catholic.

The outstanding victory that O'Connell had won in 1829 led him
and his supporters to expect another success for the same methods of
agitation. But Peel refused to be intimidated. O'Connell had virtually
defied the government to prohibit the monster meetings which he
was holding throughout the country, and the government took up
the challenge. A meeting arranged for Clontarf in October 1843 was
proclaimed on the eve of the appointed date. O'Connell cancelled it
at once and by the exercise of his great influence prevented any kind
of disturbance. This was the sensible thing to do and was strictly in
accordance with his well-known determination to avoid violence,
but nevertheless the surrender was a shock to his prestige from which
he never recovered. From this time onwards, also, he himself seemed
to lose faith in the method of agitation, and even in the cause of
repeal, and to look forward to future co-operation with the whigs
when they should return to office.

The set-back for O'Connell was of the greater importance because
his whole line of policy was at this time being challenged, actually
though not yet openly, by a nationalist movement of another stamp.
The ideas of 'ninety-eight' were in the air again and were being taken
up by a group of enthusiasts (generally known as 'Young Ireland')
who were members of the Repeal Association, but who were also

strongly influenced by the revolutionary tradition of contemporary Europe. The Young Ireland leaders had great reverence for O'Connell, as well they might, for it was he who had aroused the popular feeling which they hoped to educate, and they were anxious to work under him; but they had little patience with his determined opposition to the use of force and none at all with his clericalism. They were drawn partly from the protestant middle class, and looked for an Ireland in which men of all faiths would mingle freely; and they were willing, it seemed at times almost anxious, that it should be won by a people in arms. Their newspaper, the *Nation*, glorified the military achievements of the past and advocated military training in the present. After a good deal of suspicion and uneasiness on both sides the first open quarrel between O'Connell and the Young Irelanders came in 1845, and it is significant that it was on a religious issue. In that year Peel's government established three 'Queen's Colleges', at Belfast, Cork and Galway, to meet the need for university education in Ireland. The colleges were to be undenominational and were intended to bring together students of all creeds; O'Connell joined the Roman Catholic bishops in denouncing them as 'godless' and in condemning the policy of 'mixed education', a policy which the Young Irelanders, especially Thomas Davis, enthusiastically supported. The quarrel was followed by a formal reconciliation; but O'Connell and the bishops had their way. The Queen's Colleges of Cork and Galway, which depended on a predominantly Roman Catholic population, languished for over half a century; the college at Belfast, being accepted by the presbyterian community, had a rather happier history. The whole dispute revealed the essentially clerical character of O'Connell's nationalism; and the difference between his outlook and that of the Young Irelanders was too deep to be glossed over. In 1846 they were compelled to leave the association; and though the occasion of the separation was their refusal to renounce completely the use of physical force, this was only one aspect of a fundamental divergence. In the whole affair there was no doubt some element of personal jealousy, for an old leader can rarely endure to have his authority questioned by a new generation. But this merely strengthened the contrast between a constitutional movement backed by the church, on the one hand, and a secular and revolutionary movement on the other.

The political pattern of the 1840s was to be repeated more than half a century later, when once again a physical force party grew up within a constitutional movement and split off from it, though this time with very different results. But despite the vigorous re-emergence of the violent and revolutionary policy that he hated, it was O'Connell who gave to modern Irish nationalism its distinctive characteristics as a popular and largely clerical movement. The victories won by a revolutionary minority have only enabled it to realize these characteristics more fully.

The quarrel between O'Connell and the Young Irelanders was almost completely overshadowed by the tragedy of the Great Famine. The population had risen to over 8,000,000, about half of whom existed almost wholly on potatoes. It was a precarious state of affairs: a partial failure of the crop in 1816 had produced famine conditions over a wide area; and the fact that fever was endemic throughout the country threatened plague conditions if resistance to infection were reduced by shortage of food. Informed opinion had long been aware that the economy of Ireland was dangerously unbalanced; but no government of the period was prepared to tackle such a vast economic problem, and anyhow it was impossible to foresee a disaster of the magnitude which actually occurred or to take adequate measures against it. The famine began with a partial failure of the potato crop in the autumn of 1845; but it was the total failures during succeeding years that gave the catastrophe its unprecedented character. By 1849 the worst was over; but in the interval Ireland had lost, by death and emigration, over 1,000,000 of her people; in 1847 alone it is reckoned that almost 250,000 died of starvation or fever and over 200,000 fled to America.

During the early stages of the famine the government's policy was largely influenced by the prevalent *laissez-faire* doctrine. It set up public works, so that those in need could earn money with which to buy food; but it rejected, on principle, the idea that the government could or should undertake direct responsibility for their maintenance; and during this period the most effective relief was supplied by voluntary organizations, which received support from all parts of the world. At last, in January 1847, the government changed its policy; and by the spring of that year some 3,000,000 people were being maintained at public expense.

Landlords as well as tenants were affected by the famine. Many of them sacrificed their fortunes in an effort to save their tenantry. Others tried to insist upon their rights; and some took advantage of the occasion to clear their estates of small-holders in order to make way for farms of economic size. But, however the conduct of individual landlords may have differed, the landlord class as a whole was involved in the general impoverishment of the countryside; and the harsh conduct of some coloured the attitude of the tenants – and, indeed, of the public, in Great Britain as well as in Ireland – to the landlords in general. The Great Famine and its aftermath mark a stage in the decline of their influence.

The effect of the famine was so tremendous that it touched almost every department of life. Its most spectacular result was a rapid and permanent decline in the population, to 6,500,000 in 1851 and 5,500,000 in 1871. This decline affected mainly the rural areas, where the population sank to a level at which the land could provide a reasonable subsistence. Before the famine less than one-fifth of all agricultural holdings exceeded fifteen acres; by 1851 this proportion was already well over one half, and it was still rising. Thus a system of peasant proprietorship, which would have been impracticable in the first half of the century, eventually became at least a possible solution to the problem of landlord–tenant relationships.

The famine had also more direct and immediate effects on the course of politics. It killed the organized movements for repeal. 'The high aspirations after a national senate and a national flag had sunk to a mere craving for food': so wrote John Mitchel, the most violent of the Young Ireland party and an opponent of O'Connell's policy of constitutional agitation. The Young Irelanders' own attempt at revolution, in 1848, was a mere fiasco, for the exhaustion that followed the famine produced general apathy on political issues. O'Connell himself had died in the previous year; but the nationalist spirit that he had raised still survived; and in its recovery it was embittered by the conviction that the British government was in some way responsible, if not for the famine itself, at least for its magnitude. The steady stream of emigration, which persisted for decades, also affected the political position. It established in the United States a huge Irish population whose sense of national solidarity was based mainly on hatred of Britain, and it was among the American Irish that the tradition of violent revolution was most active. The general tendency of these political influences was to widen the already existing gap between Ulster and the rest of Ireland. The population there depended less completely on the potato and so suffered less severely from its failure than the population of the other provinces; the memory of 'black forty-seven' plays little part in Ulster tradition. Besides this, Ulster industries continued to expand, while those of the south and west, already suffering from English competition, declined more rapidly than ever. In the new Ireland which gradually emerged from the chaos of the famine years the distinctive character of the north-eastern counties was even more sharply marked than before.

The policy of home rule

The famine left Ireland politically as well as economically exhausted. The movement for repeal was dead; the Young Irelanders were scattered and discredited; no leader came forward to take O'Connell's place; Ireland had no national party and the British government had no Irish policy. Forty years later all was changed. Parnell enjoyed a supremacy no less striking, though less securely based, than that of O'Connell, and he had behind him a well-disciplined parliamentary party which comprised over eighty per cent of the Irish representation at Westminster. Instead of repeal the Irish nationalists now demanded a separate, though dependent, Irish parliament, and this policy of 'home rule' had been officially adopted by one of the two great British parties. The hope which these circumstances naturally inspired was not fulfilled. Pressure of Irish opinion secured many social reforms, but not a constitutional settlement of the political problem. This long-drawn-out failure opened the way for more vigorous and more revolutionary leadership in nationalist Ireland; and the home rule movement collapsed, after having strained the British parliamentary system almost to breaking point and dragging down with it the fortunes of the Liberal party.

The course of Irish politics in the latter half of the nineteenth century resulted, at least in part, from the government's neglect of Irish affairs in the period after the famine. While the famine lasted the miserable state of the country had aroused sympathetic concern in every part of Great Britain and large sums had been subscribed for relief. But this sympathy, already checked by the abortive insurrection of 1848, soon died away once the famine had passed. During the next two decades the attention of the British public was taken up by great events abroad – the Crimean War, the Indian Mutiny, the emergence of a united Italy, the civil war in America – and Ireland fell into the background. The attitude of government reflected that of the public. Successive ministries made some half-hearted attempts to improve the relationship between landlord and tenant; but, for the most part, they seem to have hoped that continuing emigration would bring about a gradual easing of tension. In the meantime, they saw it as their first duty to maintain law and order in a country where agrarian violence was endemic: no fewer than twelve coercion acts were passed between 1847 and 1857. It was not until the later 1860s, and then in response to a new and threatening situation in Ireland, that British politicians and the British public were prepared to give Irish affairs priority.

In the immediate aftermath of the famine, however, it had seemed that political developments in Ireland might force the government into more positive action. Many local organizations had been formed for the protection of tenants, and in 1850 these were grouped together in the Irish Tenant Right League, the so-called 'League of north and south'. This was significant as an attempt to combine Roman Catholics and protestants in a common cause, but even more significant as an experiment in using the land agitation as the basis of a national party. The League had considerable, but short-lived, success. At the general election of 1852 about forty of its nominees were returned to parliament, pledged to stand together as an independent Irish party and secure the passage of a land bill guaranteeing tenant farmers a greater degree of security in their holdings. But though united on the land question the party was liable to split on religion, which the re-establishment of a papal hierarchy in England and the consequent 'no popery' agitation had once more made a live issue in British politics. Most of the Irish Roman Catholic bishops were more concerned about this than about tenant right, which Archbishop Cullen, in particular, looked upon with suspicion as an attack on property. The party so far stuck to its principles as to reject a government measure which offered only part of what it was fighting for, but a few months later two of its most prominent leaders, despite their election pledges, accepted government office, and the Tenant Right League was hopelessly and ignominiously shattered.

But the League, despite its failure, was indicative of a significant change in the condition and outlook of the tenantry. Earlier tenant organizations had been secret and local, employing a system of terror to redress or avenge particular grievances. The League was open and national and sought to change the law by constitutional means. Agrarian terrorism certainly did not disappear; but the idea of a nation-wide campaign for legislation to restrict the power of the landlord survived and was later to prove effective. This development reflected not a worsening but an improvement in the position of the tenants. The rapid and widespread consolidation of holdings meant that a substantial majority of them now occupied farms from which they could expect to make a reasonable living. Though the repeal of the corn laws in 1846 had been followed by a fall in the price of grain, the cash value of agricultural produce in general rose between 1850 and 1870. And this rise was not matched by any general increase in rents: on many estates, indeed, rents did not rise at all during the period; and there were few estates on which the rise was equal to the rise in agricultural prices. In other words, the tenant was now receiving a larger share of the profit of his land. Except in those areas, mainly in the west, where the proportion of very small holdings was still substantial, the standard of living throughout rural Ireland showed a marked improvement. It was to safeguard this improvement, rather than to ward off destitution, that the tenants sought to weaken the power of the landlord and to make their own legal position more secure.

The practice of granting leases, normal in the eighteenth century, had declined in the nineteenth; and by the 1850s most tenants held their land on a yearly tenure. What they wanted, however, was not a return to the leasehold system, but the recognition by law of a right to retain the land they occupied so long as they paid the rent. Over most of Ulster the tenant already enjoyed this right in practice, under what was commonly called the 'Ulster custom', which, though it had no legal basis, few landlords dared to defy. Similar customs, though not so firmly established, existed in many other parts of the country; and tenants everywhere, whether or not protected by a local custom, were convinced that they had a moral right to their land. The landlord's power of eviction was always resented and sometimes resisted by force. But the government's first step towards restricting this power owed less to the tenants themselves than to a new and revolutionary force in Irish politics.

The Irish Republican Brotherhood, which formed the core of what is usually called the 'fenian' movement, was founded in 1858, but it was some years before it showed much activity. It professed to exercise authority in the name of the Irish republic. 'now virtually established', and was opposed to constitutional methods or a compromise settlement. The movement was strongest among the Irish exiles in the United States, but was established also in South Africa and Australia, and among the Irish colonies in Great Britain. In Ireland itself it was consistently opposed by the Roman Catholic church and there was little in its programme to appeal to the tenant farmer or

the agricultural labourer; though it had some thousands of supporters it was never in any sense a popular movement. Attempts at
insurrection in 1867 came to nothing, and thereafter fenianism in
Ireland steadily declined. But even in failure it exercised a considerable indirect influence on Irish opinion, and it served to remind
British statesmen, not least by its activities in England, that there
was an Irish problem to be solved. The republican tradition, though
forced into the background by its own deficiencies and by the revival
of the constitutional movement, did not disappear. It still had wide
support among Irish-Americans and through them it reacted in later
years on a nationalist Ireland which had grown tired of oratorical
politics and parliamentary manoeuvre.

The influence of fenianism on British policy appears most clearly
in the career of Gladstone. He himself had long been uneasy about
the state of Ireland; but it was not until fenian activity had aroused
public concern in Britain that he openly took up the 'Irish question';
and in 1868 he entered upon his first ministry with the famous
declaration: 'My mission is to pacify Ireland'. His first step in that
direction was to disestablish and disendow the Irish church; this
removed one of the standing grievances of the majority, and though
it aroused resentment among churchmen, it was in the main healthy
for the church herself. Gladstone's next measure, the land act of
1870, was less important for what it actually accomplished than for
its implicit acceptance of the principle that it was the government's
duty to curtail the traditional rights of the proprietor in the interests
of the tenant. In later years Gladstone's Irish policy was to be, in
appearance, much more adventurous, but the vital decision was taken
in this first ministry. By his summary treatment of the church and his
cautious, but significant, attempt to limit the authority of the landlords he was in effect destroying the basis upon which the parliamentary union had been set up and upon which it had so far been
maintained. His policy was a confession that that basis was insecure,
but subsequent experiment failed to establish any more durable
substitute.

In Ireland as in England the fenian movement had a strong effect
upon the course of politics, and by a kind of reaction helped to bring
about the establishment of a new Irish parliamentary party. The
Home Government Association, which soon became the Home Rule
League, was founded in 1870 by Isaac Butt, a protestant barrister
who had been professor of political economy in Trinity College,
Dublin. He had been a strong opponent of O'Connell's repeal

movement; and the policy he now proposed was intended, in his own view, to make the union more effective, not to dissolve it. He believed that Irish affairs were neglected at Westminster and that it would be better if they were dealt with by a subordinate parliament in Dublin. But final authority would remain with the parliament of the United Kingdom, in which Irish representation would continue unchanged. He hoped that this scheme would appeal to Irishmen of all shades of opinion – Conservative and Liberal, landlord and tenant, Roman Catholic and protestant. His optimism proved unjustified. The home rule party, though it always retained some support among protestants and landlords, soon became the party of the Roman Catholic majority and the steady advocate of the claims of the tenants. Besides this, the party's policy, however it might be limited in official pronouncements, was generally regarded, both in England and in Ireland, as an attack upon the very principle of a parliamentary union between the two countries. It was the party's alliance with the church and the tenants, and the belief that it stood for an end to English control over Ireland, that lay behind its success at the polls.

In the general election of 1874, the first to be held by secret ballot, almost sixty home-rulers were returned. They at once resolved to stand together as an independent Irish party, to press the demand for home rule, and to ally with neither government nor opposition. The formation of such a party, and a party comprising a majority of the Irish members, was a considerable achievement. As Butt put it: 'The foundation is laid for great results if we wisely and at the same time boldly use the vantage ground we have gained.' He himself, however, favoured 'wisdom' rather than 'boldness' and he made little practical use of the parliamentary party which he had created. This moderation weakened his influence in the party, though he still retained the nominal leadership; and Charles Stewart Parnell, who entered parliament in 1875, was soon recognized as the most powerful of the home rule members. Parnell was a protestant landlord, of an old and distinguished Anglo-Irish family. The chief element in his patriotism was hatred of England, learnt from his American mother, and the driving-force in his political life was love of power. Butt had tried to persuade the English by reasoned argument that Ireland should be allowed to govern herself; Parnell set out to compel them to surrender by making the existing system unworkable. He adopted and extended the method of organized obstruction which almost brought the business of parliament to a stand-still; and though the plan was in the end frustrated by the establishment of new rules of procedure, Parnell had at least forced the Irish question into a position of prominence that it would hardly have attained under Butt's milder guidance.

Butt died, broken-hearted, in 1879; and though Parnell did not succeed to the formal leadership of the party until after the general election of April 1880, he was, even before that, not only the most important of the Irish members at Westminster but also the most important political force in Ireland. The state of the country favoured the aggressive policy for which he stood. The agricultural depression of the later 1870s, which affected the whole of the British Isles, was particularly disastrous in Ireland, where the economy depended so heavily on the land. The tenant-farmers were determined to defend the higher standard of living they had achieved during the post-famine period and demanded a substantial reduction in rents, which the landlords in general resisted. The tenants found a leader in Michael Davitt, who established the Land League in October 1879, to defend their interests and, in particular, to resist evictions; and of this league Parnell became president.

The significance of this union of forces was greatly increased by an informal alliance (usually spoken of as the 'new departure') made in the same year between Parnell, Davitt and a group of American fenian leaders. These last, though they did not abandon their own belief in force, had been convinced by the effectiveness of parliamentary obstruction that it was worth while to give the constitutional home rule movement a chance; and the financial and moral support with which they provided Parnell during the succeeding years was of immense importance. But even more important was the fact that the home rule party had now quite clearly become, what Butt had never intended, a party of tenants against landlords. Almost for the first time the bulk of the people were offered a political programme of which they could see the immediate relevance to their own condition.

For the next ten years Parnell had a difficult path to follow. He had, in general, the greatest contempt for what the English might think of him, but if home rule was to be achieved by parliamentary methods he would need the help of a large section of the British electorate, and that help would be withheld unless he could convince them that he was neither encouraging violence nor condoning crime. But at the same time he had to retain the confidence of the revolutionary republicans and of the extremists of the Land League, ever ready to resent any appearance of truckling to the oppressor. His success was by no means complete, but he kept the way open for an alliance with one of the British parties while maintaining a fair degree of harmony among the various sections of his supporters. Nationalist Ireland certainly showed full confidence in him, and after the reform act of 1884, which extended household franchise to Ireland and more than tripled the electorate, the home rule party rose to eighty-six, including seventeen out of the thirty-three Ulster members. This election of 1885 marked the height of Parnell's power. He held the balance between the two British parties, for though the Liberals had a majority over the Conservatives they could not hold office if the Irish opposed them. In these circumstances Gladstone suddenly announced his conversion to a policy of self-government for Ireland; and though there were immediate signs of uneasiness among his colleagues and supporters, home rule seemed within sight. That prospect was soon shattered. In June 1886 a home rule bill was defeated by a split in the Liberal ranks, and the general election which followed left Gladstone in a hopeless minority. The nationalists maintained their numerical strength, but their freedom of action was gone, for having thrown in their lot with the Liberals they could not hope to succeed save in alliance with them.

The extent to which this alliance tied the nationalist party appears very clearly in the events of 1890. Parnell's long-standing liaison with Mrs O'Shea, the wife of one of his supporters, became public through action in the divorce courts. His party at once affirmed its continued loyalty, but the majority deserted him when it became known that Gladstone and the English Liberals thought he ought to resign. The action of the majority was strongly supported by the Roman Catholic bishops, always uneasy at protestant leadership, but it was originally dictated by English opinion. Parnell, with the help of a faithful remnant, maintained the struggle for power, and the schism in the party long survived his death in 1891. With the Liberals and the Irish nationalists weakened by internal disputes the Conservatives were able to remain almost continuously in office from 1886 to 1905. There was a brief Liberal interval from 1892 to 1895 during which Gladstone introduced a second home rule bill. It passed the commons but was rejected by the lords, who probably, on this occasion, represented pretty accurately British public opinion on the subject. When the Liberals returned to power in 1906 home rule was part of their programme; but they had at first an independent majority, and it was not until the election of January 1910 forced them to rely on on the support of the Irish members that home rule became one of the vital issues of the day.

The history of the home rule controversy suggests two closely related questions: Why were the Irish nationalists ready to accept, and why were the English so reluctant to concede, such a strictly limited measure of autonomy? In all the home rule bills the supremacy of the imperial parliament was carefully preserved, and the powers conferred upon the Irish parliament were little more than those of an extended local government. This fell far short of the repeal of the union demanded by O'Connell and meant little or nothing to the revolutionaries who were struggling for complete separation. But most home-rulers took a commonsense view of the situation. They were prepared to accept what they could get and hope for more in the future; home rule was only a first step. 'No man', said Parnell, 'has a right to fix the boundary of the march of a nation.' It was partly by emphasizing this aspect of his policy that Parnell sought to quiet the suspicions of his revolutionary allies. But many of them remained uneasy and the republican tradition survived. After his death, when the prestige of the parliamentary party declined, the movement for a violent overthrow of British rule and the establishment of a completely independent Ireland gradually gathered strength. The home rule party's relations with the Land League were simpler, for the party was always prepared to fight the cause of the tenants in parliament and in the country, and its success in this struggle did a good deal to justify it in Irish public opinion. Gladstone's second land act (1881) went far towards satisfying the claims of the tenants; and the policy of land-purchase, initiated by Gladstone, was continued and extended by the Conservatives, until Ireland was turned into a country of peasant proprietors. The Conservative party, during its long ascendancy, tried to combine strong government with a policy of 'killing home rule by kindness'; and the constant pressure of the nationalists at Westminster helped to mould the social legislation of the period in the interests of their constituents. The principles of *laissez-faire* were now abandoned. Government support was given to rural industries, to co-operative societies and for the encouragement of fisheries. Besides this, the establishment of elective county councils in 1898 took local government out of the hands of the landlords and put it under popular control. Over most of the country the home rule party could now exercise effective power, at least in local affairs; and this naturally strengthened its influence.

The English opposition to home rule is at first sight rather paradoxical. Throughout the nineteenth century Englishmen were always ready to encourage and support demands for self-government put forward by Greeks, Serbs, Italians, Magyars, Poles; and they considered it quite reasonable that British colonists in Australia, South Africa and Canada should manage their own affairs. Yet hostility to Ireland persisted; and this hostility was particularly English: the government which passed the home rule bill in 1912 depended for its majority on the votes of Irish, Scottish and Welsh members. To some extent the English attitude was dictated by obviously selfish motives: Ireland was valuable both as a market and as a source of food supply and her position made her of vital strategic importance to Britain. The various home rule bills contained safeguards on these heads, which might have satisfied legitimate anxiety; but English public opinion was opposed to the essential principle of any sort of self-government for Ireland, no matter how hedged about with conditions, and no matter how costly and inconvenient the task of keeping an unwilling partner within the union. And this opposition was maintained with a vigour, at times with an unreasoning ferocity, which formed a strange contrast to the usually calm course of English politics. English nationalism had been stirred into action, and though it might sometimes clothe itself in argument and parade as a reasoned policy, it was at bottom an irrational determination to maintain the integrity of what it regarded as the national territory and to impose its will upon every recalcitrant group within its borders.

This selfish English nationalism took some credit to itself for defending the interests of the unionist minority in Ireland, and particularly for supporting the claims of Ulster. But the Conservative party, which represented the nationalist spirit at its least scrupulous, regarded Irish unionism merely as an instrument of policy. Lord Randolph Churchill led the way. In the struggle over the first home rule bill he decided that 'the Orange card' was 'the one to play'; and during the visit to Belfast in 1886 he assured Ulster protestants that in the 'dark hour' that threatened them they would find powerful support in England. Conservative support, then and later, certainly strengthened the confidence of the Ulster protestants; but they were, in any case, resolved to defend themselves. Almost from the time at which repeal first became a serious policy they had strongly denounced it; and they were just as much opposed to the more moderate proposals for limited self-government. Their traditional fear of the Roman Catholic church, inflamed by O'Connell's clericalism, had not been appeased by the fact that Butt and Parnell were protestants and had some few protestant supporters. The composition, organization and policy of the home rule party went far to justify the protestant assertion that 'home rule is Rome rule'.

It was mainly on these grounds that almost all Irish protestants were unionists, but those of the north had another, and perhaps more cogent, argument, based on the economic position. Ireland since the union had not developed as an economic unit but as a complement to Great Britain, so that any weakening of the link would place some strain upon the poorer country. So far as the agricultural areas were concerned the balance could be fairly easily, and even profitably, adjusted; but the industries of the north would be ruined by separation. They did not exist to supply Irish needs, but formed part of the general British system, depending on Britain not only for markets but for essential supplies. The Ulster business man, apart altogether from any question of security for religion, regarded home rule as a threat to his prosperity. During the struggle over the bill of 1912 a unionist post-card, labelled 'Belfast under home rule', showed one of the principal streets overgrown with grass and a notice 'To let' stuck in front of the City Hall.

The three-cornered conflict between Britain, Ulster and nationalist Ireland reached its climax in the years immediately preceding the first world war. The house of commons passed a home rule bill in 1912; under the terms of the Parliament Act of the previous year the lords could not delay it beyond 1914, and the nationalists seemed certain of success. The opposition, however, simply intensified the struggle. Their strong point was clearly in Ulster, but while unionists in general wished to use the Ulster question to defeat home rule altogether the Ulster unionists themselves, though ready to help in this, were above all determined to protect their own interests. Their leader, Sir Edward Carson, a Dublin-born barrister and former attorney-general, was mainly concerned to save all Ireland for the union; and the true spirit of Ulster protestantism was more fully expressed by his chief lieutenant, James Craig, afterwards Lord Craigavon and first prime minister of Northern Ireland. Under their direction a provisional Ulster government was set up, 'to come into operation on the day of the passing of any home rule bill'; and a volunteer army was enrolled, drilled and armed with German rifles.

The Ulster unionists had the great advantage of being in irresponsible opposition, and the English Conservatives, from Bonar Law
downwards, gave them open encouragement to defy the authority of
parliament by every and any means. The nationalists, tied to a
nervous government, were almost helpless, for though they could
turn the Liberals out, that would bring home rule no nearer. John
Redmond, the nationalist leader, demanded in vain that the law
should be enforced. The cabinet, faced with a problem to which the
rules of parliamentary procedure offered no solution, was inclined to
wait on events, and when it did come to the point of action found to
its dismay that the army was no longer to be relied upon. Nationalist
opinion naturally became suspicious of the government's intentions
and impatient of the policy followed by Redmond and his party.
Ulster had set a better example; and there soon came into existence
another volunteer force, this time of nationalists. The bulk of them,
it is true, accepted the leadership of Redmond; but a vigorous and
influential section remained distrustful of constitutional methods.
Later they separated from the main body; and it was they who organized the insurrection of 1916, in conjunction with the socialist leader,
James Connolly, and the 'Citizen Army', which had been founded in
1913, during a prolonged labour dispute in Dublin. But the civil war
towards which Ireland seemed to be moving in the summer of 1914
was averted, temporarily, by the outbreak of a greater war in Europe.
Redmond and Carson agreed to call a truce and support the government, the home rule bill, though passed into law, was suspended for
the duration of the war, and superficial harmony was established. But,
in fact, Redmond no longer spoke for the most active and influential
section of the nationalist movement; the events of the next few years
were to destroy his leadership altogether and with it the policy of
home rule which he had brought so near success.

The end of the union

If the Ulster question had been peacefully settled, and if the home
rule act of 1914 had come into force at once, the constitutional union
between Great Britain and Ireland would have received a new lease
of life, for the act was no more than a measure of devolution and left
the parliament at Westminster, in which Ireland was still to be
represented, with undiminished supremacy. But it is not likely that
this system would have finally satisfied Irish aspirations. Already by
1914 there were forces at work which, even under home rule, would

have led to a strong, and probably irresistible, movement for virtual separation. The most important of these forces were the Gaelic revival, the republican tradition of violent revolution, the labour movement and Sinn Fein. The first, which acquired a political character from the circumstances of the time, found popular expression in two organizations: the Gaelic Athletic Association, founded by D. P. Moran in 1884 to promote traditional Gaelic games; and the Gaelic League, founded by Douglas Hyde in 1893 in order to encourage the use of the Gaelic language and to make it, eventually, the national language of Ireland. Such movements inevitably contributed, in Ireland as elsewhere, to the growth of nationalism. All that marked Ireland off as different from England strengthened the claim that she should be treated as a distinct nation, and even those who never themselves carried the argument to that point encouraged others who did. Pearse, who was one of the men chiefly responsible for the insurrection of 1916, once said that the Gaelic League was 'the most revolutionary force that has ever come into Irish history'. He was exaggerating, but it is probably true that a majority of the leaders, and even of the rank and file, in the struggle that led up to the establishment of the Irish Free State had come under its influence.

The political importance of the Gaelic League was implicit in all that it did, and the kind of outlook that it fostered was alien to the spirit of the official nationalist party. But this did not force itself upon the notice of the party leaders, who were mainly concerned to guard against any return to revolutionary methods. Superficially, all was well; for though the Irish Republican Brotherhood had been revived, the demand for a completely independent republic had not, by 1914, expressed itself in election returns, and it had little support in the country as a whole. But the notion of an appeal to force was stimulated by the resistance of the Ulster unionists. This was looked upon with admiration as a courageous refusal by Irishmen to be bound by the laws of an English parliament, and some of the more enthusiastic republicans even dreamed of an alliance with Carson against home rule, which they detested as much as he did, though on very different grounds. Admiration led naturally to imitation, and the republicans were among the most ardent of those who helped to form the Irish volunteers. For the time being, however, they were too weak to act on their own, and had to stand aside and allow Redmond to assume control of the volunteer committee. But that control was always resented by a strong minority, and in fact the whole nature and purpose of the volunteers was incompatible with the conception of home rule. Even under Redmond's unadventurous guidance they bore witness to a nationalism more enthusiastic and intransigent than his own.

Outside the narrow ranks of the Irish Republican Brotherhood, an oath-bound secret society condemned by the Roman Catholic church, republicanism was rather a sentiment, an attitude of mind, than an organized party. The most obviously active revolutionary force in Ireland in the years just before 1914 was the labour movement directed by James Connolly. The movement was essentially socialist in background and aims – its official organ was the *Workers' Republic* – but Connolly was strongly impressed by the need for the people of Ireland to control the resources of their own country before they could hope to build a socialist state, and he was prepared to fight for that independence as a necessary first step. Connolly's great importance was that he brought the urban workers over to the republican side. Since the settlement of the land problem, the driving force supplied by the grievances of the tenantry had almost disappeared and the social discontent of the towns helped to provide a substitute. It is significant that whereas the insurrections of 1798 and 1848 were rural, the only important fighting in 1916 was in Dublin. In Ireland, however, the influence of the countryside has always reasserted itself, and the workers' republic that Connolly died to establish is, to all appearance, further off now than it was then.

Connolly's effort to link the cause of Ireland with the cause of labour was not popular in his own day, and was particularly opposed by Sinn Fein. (The name 'Sinn Fein' – 'we ourselves' – was meant to indicate the policy of political and economic self-reliance advocated by the party.) This party, formally established in 1905, had grown up round a paper, *The United Irishmen*, founded some years earlier by Arthur Griffith. Griffith's object was to re-establish the constitution of 1782. He rejected violent revolution as impracticable in the circumstances of Ireland, and he condemned the constitutional methods of the parliamentary party as useless. Instead, he advocated the abstention of the Irish members from Westminster and the formation of a voluntary 'parliament' and system of arbitration courts to rule the country and maintain order by moral force. Both in the end at which he aimed and in the methods which he proposed to use Griffith was mainly inspired by the policy of the Hungarian deputies in the 1860s, and his programme was commonly spoken of as the 'Hungarian policy'. Sinn Fein was concerned with economics as well as with politics. Griffith believed that Ireland could be made self-supporting and that with proper encouragement and protection she could become an industrial as well as an agricultural country. But, though he rejected the doctrine of free trade, his economic outlook was in other respects typically nineteenth century; in particular, he had a strong respect for capital and condemned the labour movement and the strikes of 1913. In later years Sinn Fein policy was modified in many respects. The use of force was accepted, the 'Irish republic' replaced the 'constitution of 1782', and the need for reforming social conditions was recognized. The fact that Connolly at the same time was moving towards a more strongly nationalist position made possible the co-operation of the Sinn Fein and labour forces in 1916.

The year 1916 is the turning-point in the last phase of the legislative union. The outbreak of war with Germany had brought a temporary easing of the Irish situation. There was, both north and south, genuine sympathy for the allied cause. Industry and agriculture prospered. The country as a whole was prepared to wait for 'the end of the war' – the Ulster unionists with undiminished determination to resist home rule, the parliamentary nationalists with an ill-founded confidence in the willingness and ability of the British government to satisfy their claims. The small minority of separatists – republicans, socialists, Sinn Feiners – had little immediate influence on public opinion; but they drew steadily closer together and became more and more convinced that the war offered an opportunity for successful rebellion. Part of their plan was to secure German help, and negotiations were carried out by Sir Roger Casement, an Irishman and a former British colonial civil servant. But it was clear that so long as Britain had command of the sea German help, if it came at all, would be on a small scale; in the end, a project for landing arms on the coast of Kerry failed completely. Despite this, the republican leaders pressed on with their plans. They knew that they had little or no hope of immediate military success; their aim was to arouse the conscience of the people. 'There has been nothing more terrible in Irish history', wrote Pearse, 'than the failure of the last generation.' He and his colleagues believed intensely that only a sacrifice of blood could redeem that failure. The insurrection of 1916 was not the result of intolerable oppression, nor did it begin with any reasonable prospect of success; but though the fighting was over in a week the most astute political calculation could hardly have found a more effective way of arousing and uniting national sentiment.

For a very brief period it seemed as if the insurrection had failed in its purpose, for the immediate reaction of Irish nationalist opinion was to condemn it as criminal folly. But the government's treatment of the affair, however natural in the circumstances, produced an immediate revulsion of feeling. Fifteen of the insurgents were tried by court martial and shot. Had this been done immediately after the insurrection Irish opinion would probably have accepted it as a necessary protective measure by a government already fighting for its life. But the executions were dragged out over a period of several days, even after it seemed clear that the danger was over; the initiative in propaganda was left to the handful of republican sympathizers, who were encouraged and helped by the strongly anti-British attitude of the American press, and within a short time many of those who had condemned the rising were exalting its leaders as martyrs. The whole political atmosphere had suddenly changed. The uneasy suspicion with which many people had long regarded the policy of home rule turned into a burning contempt – republicanism had become the dominant political creed.

The insurrection had been mainly the work of the Irish Republican Brotherhood and the Citizen Army, but it was Sinn Fein which provided the machinery to take advantage of the rising tide of republicanism. In one by-election after another Sinn Fein candidates were returned, and the home rule party hastened its own overthrow by inflaming anti-British feeling and by an abortive experiment with the policy of abstention from attendance at parliament, which amounted almost to a confession of failure. The government's proposal to extend conscription to Ireland in 1918, though it brought about a temporary alliance of Nationalists and Sinn Feiners, really worked in favour of the latter. The anti-conscription movement, in which Roman Catholic Ireland was practically unanimous, went far to destroy the last shreds of confidence in Britain, and thus weakened still further the prestige of the parliamentary party. The effect of all this became clear in the general election of 1918. Of the hundred and five Irish seats Sinn Fein won seventy-three, the unionists twenty-six (all but three of them in Ulster), the home-rulers only six. It was a verdict against home rule rather than in favour of a republic and the result was undoubtedly influenced by wide-spread intimidation; but it marked the end of the old parliamentary nationalism and it gave Sinn Fein a claim to represent the will of the country. Before this disaster to his life's work Redmond had died, having added another name to the list of Ireland's rejected leaders.

Sinn Fein had abandoned both its objection to the use of force and its limited constitutional programme, and was now prepared to fight, if necessary, for an independent Irish republic. But it still retained a part of its 'Hungarian policy'. After the election the Sinn Fein members refused to go to Westminster; instead, they met together, assumed the title 'Dail Eireann' ('Assembly of Ireland') and declared their allegiance to the republic proclaimed by the insurgents in 1916. Eamon de Valera, the most important of the surviving 1916 leaders, was elected president, and a ministry was appointed which claimed to be the legitimate government of Ireland. The republicans placed a good deal of faith in the force of foreign opinion, especially in America, and one of their first acts was to elect delegates to the peace conference at Paris. But neither Wilson nor Clemenceau wished to embarrass the British government, and the delegates were refused recognition. The republicans were more successful at home than abroad. They dominated a majority of the various bodies which controlled local government, and in many areas voluntary arbitration courts, recognizing the authority of the Dail, exercised a far more effective jurisdiction than the courts of the crown. But such a situation could not last long without open and forcible defiance of British authority, and from the beginning of 1919 onwards armed clashes between the crown forces and the republicans became more frequent and more serious, until in July 1921 a truce was arranged as a preliminary to a permanent settlement.

Historians and politicians often refer to the events of these years as the 'Anglo-Irish war'. Ordinary people are satisfied to speak more simply, and perhaps more accurately, of the 'troubles'. The struggle was not so much between two governments or two peoples as between two largely irresponsible armed forces. The British government found the greatest difficulty in exercising effective control over the auxiliary police and the 'Black-and-Tans' (the name given to British ex-servicemen recruited into the Royal Irish Constabulary, who wore khaki uniforms with police caps and belts) on whom the bulk of the fighting fell, and the Dail had little choice but to leave the 'Irish Republican Army' to carry out operations in its own way and on its own responsibility. It was not until April 1921, when the struggle was nearly over, that de Valera, in the name of the Dail, took explicit responsibility for the war policy of the republican army. It was this lack of unified control on the Irish side that made it easy for internal disputes to develop into civil war when the British forces were withdrawn. A later generation, familiar with underground resistance movements, can appreciate the difficulties of both sides more fully than contemporaries could. The British government had the moral duty of keeping order, protecting property and maintaining some semblance of civil administration in the face of the open or concealed opposition of the great majority of the population. If they had been ready to regard Ireland as hostile territory they could easily have crushed resistance and established effective military rule; but to have done so would have been to destroy their moral right to be in the country at all. On the republican side there were all the difficulties arising from shortage of money, arms and ammunition; and all the problems facing a government carried on in secret. It has been calculated that the republican army never had more than three thousand men in action at once, and they were quite incapable of undertaking regular military operations, for which, indeed, there was little opportunity in a war without a frontier. Their methods were ambushes, assassinations and raids. They wore no uniform and could easily emerge from and disappear into the civilian population. The crown forces, driven almost to distraction by the attacks of a ruthless and elusive enemy, adopted a policy of reprisals, sometimes with, sometimes without, the approval of the authorities. It was a war in which victory was impossible. The British might have restored order, but they could not have established the state of mutual confidence necessary for democratic government. The republicans could and did make normal administration impossible, but they could never, in their own strength, have driven the British out. The main factor in bringing the war to an end was not the force of arms, but the force of British public opinion. What the war did accomplish was the preparation of both sides for a compromise.

The necessity for compromise, implicit from the beginning in this as in most other struggles, was emphasized by the position of Ulster. Unionism as a serious political force had disappeared from the rest of Ireland, but in Ulster it was stronger than ever; and the claims and methods of the republican forces went far towards making a united Ireland impossible. The British government, anxious for some sort of settlement as speedily as possible, had passed, in 1920, the Government of Ireland Act, which made provision for two Irish parliaments, one in the north and the other in the south. The northern parliament, with its seat at Belfast, was to legislate for the six counties of Antrim, Armagh, Down, Fermanagh, Londonderry and Tyrone, which together had a protestant majority, though Roman Catholics, concentrated for the most part in particular areas, formed a very considerable minority. A parliament at Dublin was to legislate for the rest of the country, and a 'Council of Ireland' was to consider matters of common interest. The powers of the two parliaments were to be similar to those conferred by the home rule act of 1914 and Irish representation at Westminster was to continue. As a result of this act the new state of Northern Ireland came into existence in 1921.

This safeguarding of the Ulster unionists was the main result of the act; for it had no chance of acceptance in the south, where the struggle continued as before. The republicans made great efforts to prevent the northern government from functioning. Even before that government had come into existence Belfast and some other areas in Ulster had been seriously disturbed by sectarian riots, in which the Roman Catholics, as the weaker party, had suffered heavily. But now a concerted effort, organized by IRA headquarters, was made to disrupt civil administration altogether, and the initial refusal of the Roman Catholic population to co-operate in working the constitution of the new state laid them open to suspicion of complicity in the republican campaign. The Northern Ireland government, with British military resources to back it up, was able to restore order and establish its authority, but the long and bitter struggle left an enduring mark on the character of the regime.

The British government, having salved its conscience with regard to Ulster, was anxious for a compromise with the republicans. Foreign opinion, especially in the United States, was increasingly hostile, and the task of convincing a sceptical world of the justice of Britain's claims in Ireland was becoming almost impossible. At home, there was public uneasiness about the object and the methods of a war which seemed to be fought against the very principle of self-determination. The stories published in the newspapers might be exaggerated, partial and ill-informed, but the conscience of the country was stirred and refused to be satisfied with the answer that the atrocities of the republicans exceeded those of the Black-and-Tans. The republicans, for their part, were ready to welcome a respite. Their ranks were depleted by casualties and captures, they were finding it increasingly difficult to obtain arms and ammunition, and the country was getting tired of the fighting. When Lloyd George's invitation to negotiate came, rather suddenly, in June 1921, they were almost at the end of their resources. Early next month a truce was arranged, and the work of finding a compromise began.

The history of the negotiations, which extended over severa months, is a confused one and, on the Irish side, a subject of bitter dispute. But from the beginning the essence of the position was clear to all men of common sense: both sides must make substantia concessions, and the only alternative to a settlement was a renewal of war. Lloyd George had explicitly stated that Ireland could not be allowed to sever herself completely from the British Empire and that Ulster must not be coerced. These conditions being accepted, every other subject was open for discussion. The leaders of the Irish delegation, Arthur Griffith and Michael Collins, were essentially practical men. Griffith had always disliked the use of force and was mainly interested in economic and administrative problems. He saw in Lloyd George's offer of dominion status an approach to his own 'Hungarian policy', and he was at least partly responsible for inducing his colleagues to accept it. Collins had played a leading part in the struggle of the previous two years and had won a great reputation for courage and skill; he knew how precarious the position of the republican forces was and how difficult it would be to continue if the British government chose to exert its full strength. In these circumstances a treaty* was signed on 6 December 1921. Ireland was to become a self-governing dominion of the British Commonwealth, under the style of the 'Irish Free State', and was specifically guaranteed the same degree of constitutional independence as the dominion of Canada. In practice, this did not fall far short of a republican settlement; but there were three limitations which the Irish delegates had accepted very reluctantly: members of parliament were to take an oath of allegiance to the crown, in virtue of Ireland's membership of the British Commonwealth; Northern Ireland was to be left free, if it chose, to stay out of the new dominion and continue its existing constitutional position within the United Kingdom; the British government retained peace-time naval establishments in certain Irish ports. It was on the first of these conditions that the debate turned when the terms came to be debated in the Dail. De Valera himself, who had taken no direct part in the later stages of the negotiations, led the attack and supported it with all the glamour of his reputation and all the emotional force of an appeal to the inviolable rights of the republic. Griffith, the mainstay of the defence, was a less romantic figure. He ignored juridical subtleties and emotional appeal, and

*On the British side the official term is 'articles of agreement', but 'treaty' is in much more common use, and on the Irish side has always been insisted upon, as implying the sovereign status of the republican government.

onfined himself to the common-sense line of argument that he and
his colleagues had been sent to London 'not as republican doctrin-
ires, but looking for the substance of freedom and independence';
that the treaty, in spite of many defects, did give that substance, and
hat it need not be regarded as a final settlement. After long and bitter
debates, which lasted until 7 January 1922, the treaty was accepted by
he Dail, and a week later a provisional government under Michael
Collins was set up to take over authority from the British. There
vere further formalities to be gone through; but the legislative union,
after its hundred and twenty years of uneasy existence, had, in fact,
come to an end.

To Irish nationalists the legislative union is a period of oppression
and degradation, to the Irish unionists a great experiment which
went wrong; to the historian its main characteristic is that it made
possible the Irish nation of today. By surrendering their political
independence in 1800 the protestant landlords gained a temporary
security for their privileges but lost the power to defend them for
the future, and the gradual destruction of those privileges by successive British governments left the way open for the rise of the Roman
Catholic peasantry and middle class to a dominant position. In
1800, the alternative to union seemed to be either the survival of an
intransigent protestant ascendancy or its replacement by a revolutionary Ireland, governed according to the principles of French
enlightenment. It was the peace imposed by Britain that made possible
the emergence of a third force, the Roman Catholic nation, which
was sustained by protestant leadership and revolutionary fervour,
but was strong enough to keep its own character against both. 'When
I was a boy', said one of the Beresfords in the mid-nineteenth century,
' "the Irish people" meant the protestants, now it means the Roman
Catholics.' The social and political transformation that this implies
was, for good or ill, the most enduring legacy of the union.

6 From the treaty to 1972

The legislative union had been established in the middle of a desperate war, and the main motive on the British side had been military security. Its dissolution came after an even greater war had been brought to a victorious conclusion and at a time when peace and self-confidence made British public opinion particularly disposed towards a generous settlement. There was, therefore, in 1921 and 1922 a serious desire to meet the needs and claims of Ireland, a desire that had been almost completely lacking in 1800. Yet in spite of this contrast both the union and its dissolution suffered from the same defect, in that both failed to solve the two radical problems that stood in the way of a permanent and peaceful settlement of Irish affairs: the internal problem of relations between Roman Catholic and protestant, and the external problem of relations between Ireland and Great Britain. The Government of Ireland Act and the treaty changed the form but not the substance of these problems. The old conflict of interests between the protestant ascendancy and the Roman Catholic masses had gone, but it was replaced by the political division between Northern Ireland, with its predominantly protestant population, and the rest of the country; and within Northern Ireland mutual fears and suspicions kept sectarian conflict alive. This situation in turn left an element of uneasiness in Anglo-Irish relations. The two countries were, however, bound closely together by a common economic interest; and this link, though resented by some Irishmen as essentially a continuation of British imperialism, was so strong that no Dublin government could afford permanently to ignore it. The failure of the treaty settlement to bring complete harmony to Anglo-Irish relations was in some measure qualified by the operation of economic forces.

The signing of the treaty did not put an immediate end to the fighting in Ireland. In the north, the IRA campaign against the new regime continued, even after Collins had agreed, in March 1922, to call off his forces. In the rest of the country, disagreement over the terms of the treaty led, within a few months, to the outbreak of a civil war. The first reaction to the treaty had, indeed, been one of relief; but doctrinaire republicanism was strong both in the IRA and among the political leaders. Though the Dail approved the treaty, after a long and acrimonious debate, and though a general election in June 1922 returned a pro-treaty majority, the republican die-hards refused to accept this verdict. On the political side, their opposition was organized by de Valera; on the military side, they had the support of a large section of the IRA – it was, indeed, the division in the army rather than among the politicians or in the country at large that led directly to civil war. The new Free State government, under Arthur Griffith and Michael Collins, was at first reluctant to force the issue; but the aggressive action of their opponents left them no alternative, and by the end of June open hostilities had broken out.

The republicans now used against the Free State all the methods which in previous years had been used against the British. They could no longer, however, count on the same public support, and their wholesale destruction of property and frequent bank-robberies, together with the suspicion that they favoured a communist land-policy, turned a population heartily sick of rule by revolver more and more against them. Besides this, the new government showed energy, determination and courage, and, above all, a ruthlessness that the British had never dared to display.* They executed scores of prisoners and left hunger-strikers to starve if they chose. These measures had their effect, and in May 1923 de Valera announced the end of resistance. But it was beyond his power to control the forces that years of irregular warfare had unloosed, and the threat of violence remained part of the background of Irish political life.

The civil war had had the effect of easing republican pressure on the north, and there also the effective authority of government had been established by 1923. The struggle in the north had, inevitably, followed sectarian lines. To the protestants, the separate status of the six-county area was the only guarantee against domination by a Dublin parliament. To the Roman Catholics, it meant condemnation to the position of a permanent minority. Naturally enough, many of them gave active support to the republican attack; and throughout

*Miss Macardle, in her republican apologia, lists forty republicans executed by the British between 1916 and 1921, and seventy-seven executed by the Free State government in 1922 and 1923. D. Macardle, *The Irish republic* (London, 1927), pp. 1023–5.

the province it was in the predominantly Roman Catholic areas that the republicans had their strongholds. Ulster protestants had long believed that Roman Catholics were essentially 'disloyal'; they regarded the events of the early 1920s as confirmation of this belief; and when peace was at length restored the prospects of reconciliation between the two sections of the population seemed further off than ever. The old equations of 'protestant' with 'unionist' and of 'Roman Catholic' with 'nationalist' still stood; and in the confined area of Northern Ireland these equations were bound to have a stultifying effect on political life.

Decade after decade the leaders, on both sides, stuck to their traditional attitudes. The main object of the unionists was to make sure that every protestant voter supported the unionist party; and they hardly even thought of trying to broaden its scope by an appeal to the minority. The nationalists were no less sectarian. They based themselves exclusively on those areas that were predominantly Roman Catholic, and nationalist MPs regarded the defence of Catholic interests as their main function. So complete and so rigid was the division that there was no room for any third force. A struggling labour party, itself split over the question of partition, did succeed in returning a few members to parliament; but their presence there did not change the general character of the situation.

There was nothing new in this sectarianism, which had existed for generations. What was new, since 1920, was that the protestants now had continuous control of the organs of administration; and they used this control, together with the influence they derived from their economic superiority, to make sure that their own predominance and their majority position should continue indefinitely. A Roman Catholic seeking employment, or housing, or advancement in his career, generally found himself at a heavy disadvantage in competition with protestants; and for many the only escape lay in emigration: though the birth-rate among Roman Catholics was higher than among protestants, the Roman Catholic proportion of the population showed little increase during the first forty years of the Northern Ireland regime. From the unionist viewpoint, this general distrust of Roman Catholics was justified on the grounds of their attitude in the past and their continued support for the merging of Northern Ireland with the rest of the country under the Dublin government. But, whatever the force of this argument, there was little in the policy of the unionist party that might induce the northern nationalists to change their views and accept the existing situation as final. The peace established in the early 1920s had only strengthened and embittered the rivalry between the opposing groups. On both sides, the leaders were men whose views had been hardened during the fierce controversy over home rule. The first prime minister of Northern Ireland was Sir James Craig (created Viscount Craigavon in 1927), who had been Carson's principal lieutenant; and the chief representative of the nationalist minority was Joseph Devlin, formerly a prominent member of the Home Rule party. Though they were men of long experience and basic common sense, they had little freedom of manoeuvre: Craig could not escape from the position in which the unionists had entrenched themselves in the early 1920s; and Devlin was the spokesmen of the Catholic minority rather than the effective leader of an organized political movement.

In the south, also, the events of those years had a continuing influence, for political attitudes were long determined by the divisions established during the civil war. Thus, in both parts of the country, normal political development was hampered; and the electorate was often more easily moved by the invocation of men and movements of the past than by any consideration of the actual circumstances in which everyday life had to be lived.

This virtual stagnation of politics survived so long mainly because of the importance attached by all parties to the question of partition. It is true that this had not been a major issue in the civil war; but both sides in that struggle had believed that the question would soon settle itself. The treaty had provided for a modification of the boundary between Northern Ireland and the rest of the country; and nationalists of all shades of opinion were convinced that the result would be the speedy disappearance of Northern Ireland as a separate political unit. In fact, however, when a boundary commission was later set up it accomplished nothing; and in 1925 the existing boundary was accepted as definitive by the governments of the United Kingdom, Northern Ireland and the Irish Free State. But, despite this, successive Dublin governments continued to demand the ending of partition and the inclusion of the six-county area under their jurisdiction. While this was the prevailing attitude in Dublin the northern unionist was not likely to feel secure, nor was the northern nationalist likely to give up hope; and neither was likely to accept the necessity for compromise.

Though the question of partition was thus a central one, it would be a mistake to suppose that partition itself was the cause of the unhealthy state of Irish politics. Partition was not a cause, but a symptom. It had been imposed by a British government as a means of solving an age-old problem; and, though it had failed in its purpose, the problem would not now be solved, even if its form would be changed, by a mere reversal of policy. The forced inclusion of the northern protestants in an all-Ireland state could lead only to a civil war, the ferocity and destructiveness of which it is easy to imagine, but to the duration of which no likely limit could be foreseen. Some observers were impressed by the fact that the protestant minority in the south had accepted the new regime there, and had been well treated by the government. But the southern protestants were too small a body to be politically significant; and, in any case, their numbers had declined sharply and continuously since the establishment of the Free State, and they seemed doomed to disappear almost completely within a few generations. The strongly knit and growing protestant population in the north was in a very different position.

The partition question, however stultifying its influence, was often useful to politicians on both sides of the border, and they never allowed the electorate to forget it for long. But, at the same time, the routine business of government had to go on; and during the half-century that followed the treaty Ireland had to be guided through great social and economic changes. For Northern Ireland, as an integral part of the United Kingdom, all major decisions were taken at Westminster; and the Northern Ireland government could have only a marginal influence on the shaping of the total economy. Within fairly narrow limits, however, it could and did take the initiative: its agricultural policy produced an enormous improvement in the standard of farming; and its constant efforts to introduce new industries helped to reduce the traditional dependence on textiles, engineering and shipbuilding, all of which were tending to decline. In social legislation it had greater freedom of action; but the unionists adopted a 'step by step' principle, which meant that Northern Ireland followed British example fairly closely. There were some local variations, due partly to the special circumstances of the province and partly to the very conservative outlook of the unionist leadership; but, broadly speaking, economic and social development in the north followed the British model. There was, in fact, little opportunity, even if there had been the desire, to reshape society on new and independent lines. In the south, it was very different. Though the conflict over the terms of the treaty remained, even after 1923, as the major political issue, the life of the country was far more profoundly affected by economic and social changes on which all parties were in broad agreement.

The Free State had emerged from the civil war under new leadership: Griffith died in 1922 and Collins was killed in an ambush in the same year. The new head of the government was W. T. Cosgrave, a quietly efficient administrator. He was without the vigour and force of character of Collins, who had been his predecessor, or of de Valera, who was to follow him; but he retained office for ten troublesome years and he gave the new state a respectable stability that it might not have acquired under more adventurous guidance. The outstanding member of his cabinet was Kevin O'Higgins, minister for justice, whose stern measures of repression helped to stamp out political crime, though they also led to his own assassination in 1927. But the same year saw a long step towards the establishment of normal political conditions. De Valera and his followers, though numerically the strongest of the opposition parties, had hitherto been excluded from the Dail by their refusal to take the oath of allegiance prescribed in the treaty; now they changed their attitude, in fact if not in theory, and, after a general election in 1927, they took their seats.* Their advent weakened the position of the Cosgrave government, which now had to rely on the support of other parties; but it had already laid down clearly the lines along which future policy was to develop.

In this policy three principal objects can be distinguished: first, to weaken the constitutional connection with Britain and to emphasize the sovereign independence of the state; secondly, to encourage manufacturing industry, and thus reduce dependence upon imports from Britain; thirdly, to promote the 'Gaelicization' of Irish society. In pursuing the first of these objects the Cosgrave government confined itself within the limits imposed by the treaty. Thus, for example, it took an important share in the discussions leading up to the Statute of Westminster, by which the sovereign status of the dominions was formally recognized; but it refused to abolish the oath of allegiance. At the same time, however, it was careful to insist that its relations with the crown should be direct and formal, and in no way controlled or supervised by the British government. But all this was, in reality, little more than a matter of prestige. The policies

*Not all the anti-treaty forces accepted de Valera's policy of entering the Dail. Those who did so were organized in a new political party under the title Fianna Fail. The Cosgrave party was known as Cumann na nGaedheal, later changed to Fine Gael.

followed at home had far greater importance, both immediately and for the future.

Griffith had looked forward to political independence as a means of establishing economic independence also; and, true to his principles, the Free State government had quickly imposed a wide range of protective tariffs. As a result, some new industries were set up; and some British manufacturers, anxious to keep their place in the Irish market, established subsidiary companies in Ireland. But there was a lack of capital and experience; and, in any case, the Irish and British economies were so closely intermingled, and the predominance of Britain so strongly established, that fundamental changes in the situation were hardly possible without a much more revolutionary policy than any Irish government was likely to venture on. The efforts of the Cosgrave government and its successors were certainly not fruitless; and the economy became gradually more diversified. But the dream of an Ireland with large and expanding manufactures and a steadily growing population remained no more than a dream.

If the economic policy of the Free State was derived from Griffith, its cultural policy was inspired by Pearse, whose ideal had been an Ireland 'not free only, but Gaelic as well'. It now became the aim of government to Gaelicize every aspect of Irish life and, more especially, to extend the use of the Irish language. It was made an essential part of the curriculum in all schools subsidized by the state, and great encouragement was given to the teaching of other subjects through the medium of Irish. A knowledge of it was required from all civil servants; and it was given official status in government documents and publications. But the policy had little obvious success: English remained the language of ordinary life everywhere except in those remote western areas which had an unbroken Gaelic-speaking tradition. Yet even the obligation to learn the language had its effect; and this was strengthened by the emphasis constantly laid on what were considered the essentially Gaelic elements in Irish history and tradition. Thus, even people who rarely spoke Irish and who, perhaps, understood it very imperfectly, nevertheless became accustomed to the idea of a Gaelic distinctiveness. This fell far short of Pearse's ideal; but it marked a real change in what one might call the cultural atmosphere.

These policies, inaugurated by the Cosgrave administration, were continued and extended by its successor. After the general election of 1932 de Valera's Fianna Fail was the largest single party, though without an absolute majority in the Dail. There was, however, sufficient support from minor groups to enable de Valera to form a government, and he entered upon a period of office that lasted continuously until 1948.

The most striking characteristic of this long period was a steady weakening of the British connection. De Valera was not restrained, as his predecessor had been, by regard for the terms of the treaty; and one of the first acts of his government was to remove the oath of allegiance from the constitution. Almost at the same time he became involved in a dispute with Britain over payments to be made by the Free State under the terms of financial agreements concluded in 1923 and 1926 (the most important of these payments consisted of the annuities still being collected under the terms of the various land-purchase acts). When these payments were withheld in 1932 the British government retaliated by imposing tariffs on Free State goods imported into the United Kingdom; and the dispute developed into an 'economic war'. The Free State government used this as an opportunity to intensify the policy of economic self-sufficiency, and also made great efforts to direct the country's overseas trade away from the United Kingdom; but, though it was fairly easy to find alternative sources of supply for goods formerly imported from Britain, it proved almost impossible to find any other market for Irish exports. Thus the policy of economic separation from Britain had no more than a partial and somewhat precarious success. The concomitant policy of constitutional separation achieved more permanent results. In 1936 the Free State government took advantage of the abdication of Edward VIII to pass the External Relations Act, which practically removed the crown from the constitution, except for formal diplomatic purposes. A further step was taken in the following year, with the promulgation of an entirely new constitution, which was in all essential respects republican and not monarchical, though the term 'republic' was not used and though the crown still retained the functions allotted to it by the act of 1936. Much more significant was the fact that the constitution claimed to be a constitution for the whole island: the term 'Irish Free State' was abandoned and 'Ireland' (Eire) substituted.* The British government rejected the idea that this claim could affect the existing constitutional position of Northern Ireland; but, in other respects, it was prepared to recognize the new constitution. Both sides were, in fact, now

*The constitution was published both in Irish and in English. In the English version the name of the state is given as 'Ireland'; but in normal English usage the Irish name 'Eire' was used to indicate the twenty-six counties.

anxious to settle their differences; and in 1938 Chamberlain and de Valera reached a comprehensive agreement. The financial dispute was settled by a compromise; and the British government undertook to withdraw its forces from the 'treaty ports', where it had maintained establishments since 1921 – a concession of which the full importance was soon to be revealed when the United Kingdom became involved in the second world war.

The neutrality of Eire during this war was a clear demonstration of the extent and reality of her separation from Britain and the rest of the Commonwealth. But neutrality was, in the circumstances, a natural policy to follow, for the reasons that had forced upon Britain a tardy decision to resist German aggression did not affect Eire with anything like the same urgency. Besides, there was still an active group of republican extremists who had never accepted de Valera's decision to adopt constitutional means; they maintained a military organization, 'the Irish Republican Army' (IRA), and they regarded England as the only enemy. Any attempt to bring Eire into the war on the allied side could have provoked such widespread and violent resistance that government might well have been paralysed. A state built upon revolutionary principles can rarely afford to run such risks, and neutrality was probably the safest policy to follow. For Britain, now that she had given up the treaty ports, this neutrality meant a dangerous weakening of her western defences; and the government in London seriously considered occupying Eire by force. Only the fact that Northern Ireland was still part of the United Kingdom made it possible to refrain from this action without fatally exposing overseas communications. It was thus the partition of Ireland that enabled the greater part of the country to escape the full rigours of war, though thousands of volunteers from Eire did, in fact, join the British forces.

Eire's neutrality provided the northern unionists with another justification of their refusal to leave the United Kingdom; but long before this the whole trend of de Valera's policy had confirmed them in their belief that they had little common ground with the bulk of their fellow-countrymen. Their economy was so closely tied to that of Great Britain that they could not afford to have tariff barriers set up; and the steady whittling away of the constitutional connection destroyed any likelihood of their being able to enter a united Ireland which would be an active and cooperative member of the British Commonwealth. But, apart altogether from this, there were elements in the policy pursued by Dublin governments since 1922 that seemed, at least to northern protestants, to indicate an intention of turning Ireland into an essentially Gaelic and Catholic state. The language policy inaugurated in the 1920s was continued even more energetically, though with little more appearance of success, under de Valera. So far as religion was concerned, the government's attitude was, at first, one of formal neutrality; though the denial of the right of civil divorce, in 1925, suggested a readiness to bring the law of the state into line with Roman Catholic teaching. But a new policy was made explicit in the constitution of 1937, which accorded a special status to the Roman Catholic church. These policies were quite appropriate to the twenty-six-county area; and here, though they aroused some criticism, they met no serious opposition. But they were put forward specifically as policies for all Ireland and for all Irishmen; and, as such, they were seen by northern unionists as a clear indication of the kind of treatment they might expect if the country were to be re-united.

When one considers the attitudes of the two Irish governments one can hardly help observing that, however much they might differ in other respects, they shared a common insensitiveness to minority opinion. The government in Belfast administered Northern Ireland as if the whole population should conform to (or, at least, accept as normal) the patterns imposed by the protestant and unionist majority. The government in Dublin planned the new and united Ireland to which it looked forward on the implicit assumption that the northern protestants would have to abandon their distinctive characteristics and be submerged in a predominantly Gaelic and Catholic community. Wolfe Tone might be denounced in the north and idolized in the south; but his principles were disregarded equally in both parts of the country.

De Valera did not give formal expression to the spirit of his policy by declaring a republic, perhaps because he hesitated to break the last link, however tenuous, with the other nations of the Commonwealth. His failure to do so increased the resentment with which he was regarded by republican extremists, and was one of the factors that led to his defeat in the general election of February 1948, though this was mainly due to the natural reaction of public opinion after sixteen years of government by one party or, rather, by one man, for de Valera had dominated both Fianna Fail and the country. After the election Fianna Fail, though still the largest party in the Dail, no longer had a majority; and the desire for a change of government was so general and so strong that all the other parties, despite the opposing programmes on which they had fought the election, joined in a coalition held together by no common principle except that of keeping de Valera out of office.

To the surprise of most, and the consternation of many, this new government decided to take the final step in the process of separation. In September 1948 the prime minister, J. A. Costello, then on a visit to Ottawa, announced that legislation would shortly be introduced to sever the last constitutional link between Eire and the Commonwealth by repealing the External Relations Act. Before the end of the year this had been done; and on Easter Monday 1949 the republic was formally inaugurated. The change, which was generally recognized as one of name only, aroused little enthusiasm in Ireland and no resentment in Britain. The removal of the crown from the constitution made no practical difference; and in other respects everything went on as before. By arrangement between Dublin and London, citizens of the republic were not to be treated as aliens in the United Kingdom, nor British citizens as aliens in the republic. Though the diplomatic representatives exchanged by the two governments now became 'ambassadors' instead of 'high commissioners', Irish affairs continued to be dealt with by the Commonwealth Relations Office, so long as it retained a separate existence. It is, perhaps, hardly surprising that the IRA and its supporters refused to accept the republic of 1949 as a substitute for the republic of 1916, to which alone they professed allegiance; and the new regime, like its predecessors, had to face the recurrent threat of internal violence.

The course of events had been watched with great anxiety in the north. Though the constitutional change had been so much a matter of form, the Dublin government had used the occasion to reiterate its claim to authority over the whole island and had launched a vigorous propaganda campaign against partition, accompanied by bitter denunciations of the unionist party. The effect on Northern Ireland of the propaganda was demonstrated at a general election in February 1949, when the appearance of anti-partition candidates subsidized from the south led only to an increase in the unionist vote and a strengthening of the government's position in parliament. What the unionists really feared, however, was the effect of propaganda in Britain. Since 1945, they had had to deal, almost for the first time, with a Labour government at Westminster; and not only was Labour traditionally sympathetic to Irish nationalism, but there were many constituencies where Labour members depended heavily on the votes of Irish immigrants. In fact, however, unionist fears proved groundless; and the legislation passed by the British parliament in 1949 to regulate relations with the new republic expressly provided that no change should be made in the constitutional status of Northern Ireland without the consent of the Northern Ireland parliament.

In one respect, 1949 marked the end of a period: so far as the twenty-six-county area was concerned, the treaty of 1921 had now been reversed, the last symbol of British authority removed, and the country left completely free to go its own way. But there remained the question of partition. From the British point of view, this was a matter to be settled between north and south: if the parliament of Northern Ireland expressed a wish to enter the republic no difficulty would be made. But the government of the republic saw the situation differently. It insisted that partition was imposed by Britain; and refused either to recognize the constitutional status of Northern Ireland or to admit that the Northern Ireland parliament had any right to determine the future of the province. This divergence of outlook had, however, little practical effect on Anglo-Irish relations. The republic constantly advertised its sense of grievance; but it either would not or could not take any positive action; and the partition question gradually acquired an air of unreality. Political leaders in the republic continued to talk about it; but in practice they accepted the existing situation and acted as if it were to last indefinitely.

This acquiescent attitude was, of course, condemned by the extreme republican groups, of which the IRA was the most important. But their own efforts met with such ill-success that they merely served to show how the political atmosphere was changing. During the 1950s they maintained a sporadic campaign of terrorism in the north, only to find themselves condemned both by the leaders of the northern nationalists, to whom they might have looked for support, and by public opinion in the south, where the government took strong measures to suppress their activities. It seemed, now, as if old quarrels were dying and as if Ireland might move, even if slowly, towards some sort of stability based upon the *status quo*.

The mere passage of time contributed to this development. By 1960 the border had been in existence for forty years, and the effect, on both parts of the country, of such a long period of separation could not be unfelt. But there were other influences also. Constitutional independence had not altered the fact that Ireland was part of the British economic system.* The attempt to break away from this in

*In 1960 the total value of exports from the republic was *c.* £152 million. Of this, *c.* £91 million went to Great Britain; *c.* £19 million to Northern Ireland;

the 1930s had failed; and during the 1950s and 1960s successive governments in Dublin had shown themselves not only ready to accept the situation but increasingly anxious for closer integration. In 1965 when Fianna Fail was once more in office, under de Valera's successor, Sean Lemass, a comprehensive commercial treaty was concluded with Britain. This provided for a progressive reduction of tariffs on both sides, and was meant to lead to the establishment of an Anglo-Irish free-trade area by 1975.

The republican government's readiness to strengthen economic links with Britain without pressing the question of partition reflects its general attitude at this period. The claim to jurisdiction over the six-county area was not abandoned, or even modified; but it gradually fell into the background both with politicians and with the public at large. This change of attitude in the south contributed to a gradual easing, already apparent, of internal tensions in the north. Among unionists, there was a growing body who believed that the constitution could be maintained without constant reliance on the old sectarian battle-cries and that some greater effort should be made to win the co-operation of the minority in efforts for the common good. Among Roman Catholics, there was more readiness than in the past to seek and welcome opportunities for such co-operation. Though most of them still held to the ideal of a united Ireland, there were many who felt that it could not be attained in the foreseeable future, and that they should therefore accept the existing situation and make the best of it. On both sides, these more friendly attitudes were encouraged by the contemporary spirit of ecumenism, which affected Ireland, as it affected the rest of Christendom.

A change in the Northern Ireland government in 1963 marked a critical stage in this development. The retiring prime minister, Lord Brookeborough, had held office since 1941, and was regarded, perhaps rather unfairly, as an embodiment of the old-fashioned unionism inherited from the conflict of the early 1920s. His successor, Captain Terence O'Neill, was a much younger man, more alert to present opportunities and future developments than to fears inherited from the past. He emphasized the need not only for a policy of reconciliation at home but for the establishment of closer relations

---

c. £11 million to the USA (the republic's third best customer). The value of the republic's imports was *c.* £226 million, of which *c.* £104 million came from Great Britain and *c.* £13 million from Northern Ireland. (In the same year, the total value of exports from Great Britain was *c.* £3 billion and from Northern Ireland *c.* £335 million.)

with the south; and, in pursuance of this, he arranged an exchange of visits with the prime minister of the republic. For a time, it seemed as if a new era of peace and good-will was at hand.

But any attempt to change established patterns of political behaviour is bound to be perilous. For forty years, unionist leaders had appealed to the prejudices of protestants and had done what they could to curtail the political influence of Roman Catholics; they could not now alter their course without arousing dangerous fears on one side and no less dangerous expectations on the other. The rank-and-file of the unionist party saw in O'Neill's policy a threat to their own monopoly of power; and the Roman Catholics became more and more insistent that expressions of good-will should be translated into positive reforms, especially in the field of local government, which had hitherto been carefully organized so as to exclude them from effective control, even in areas where they formed a majority of the population. Almost suddenly, what had seemed a hopeful situation became one of violent conflict. Fear on one side and impatience on the other frustrated the efforts of those who had hoped for the gradual development of mutual understanding and confidence.

From the beginning of O'Neill's premiership his attitude had caused alarm among some right-wing unionists, and this alarm had found a militant spokesman in Ian Paisley, a protestant preacher who had established a new sect calling itself the Free Presbyterian Church of Ulster. He appealed simultaneously to fears of a 'Romeward trend', which he claimed to detect in the older denominations, and to suspicions of a Catholic conspiracy to drag Northern Ireland into the republic; and the popular response that he aroused in some quarters certainly influenced many MPs who were formally committed to supporting the prime minister's policy. On the other side, those who demanded immediate reforms organized themselves, after American example, in a Civil Rights movement, and conducted a series of marches and demonstrations. In the course of 1968 the two groups clashed more than once, both with each other and with the police; and a major riot in Londonderry in October inaugurated a prolonged period of civil disorder.

As violence spread, there was a significant change of tone. To begin with, the Civil Rights movement had had considerable protestant support, and it had concentrated on the need for certain specific reforms, in particular, an extension of the local government franchise. But it soon became in fact, though not in principle, a sectarian body;

and its aims became both vaguer and more extensive. Many of its members, and many of the groups and organizations associated more or less closely with it, were not now likely to be satisfied by any reforms within the existing constitutional framework. They were in general agreement that unionism must be totally destroyed; and those among them who disclosed any constructive plans for the future favoured, for the most part, a workers' republic on the pattern put forward, more than half a century earlier, by James Connolly.

In face of this situation, right-wing influence in the unionist party grew stronger, and O'Neill's leadership came under heavy attack. In a general election, in February 1969, he tried to rally public opinion behind a programme of moderate reform; but the result did nothing to improve his position, and a few months later he was forced out of office, and succeeded by Major James Chichester-Clark, a former member of his cabinet. The change of leadership did not, however mean a change of policy. By this time, indeed, a change of policy was virtually impossible. The government at Westminster, where Labour was in office, had become deeply concerned about the situation in Northern Ireland and had made it clear that the programme of reform announced by O'Neill must be speedily completed. Under the terms of the Government of Ireland Act, the Westminster parliament possessed the constitutional powers necessary to give effect to this decision; but, in practice, recourse to these powers was not likely to be necessary, for the economic and financial dependence of Northern Ireland on the rest of the United Kingdom was such that no government there could hope to function satisfactorily in defiance of the government in London. The fact that the Conservative opposition at Westminster was equally insistent on the necessity for reforms in Northern Ireland made the isolation of the right-wing unionists complete.

The fall of O'Neill had been followed by several weeks of comparative tranquillity. But the extremists on both sides were preparing to renew the struggle; and in August fresh fighting broke out on a scale that the police could not hope to control. The British government now sanctioned the use of troops; the forces normally stationed in Northern Ireland were rapidly expanded; and with this help order was restored. But it was clear that the peace was precarious and that its maintenance would depend, for an indefinite period, on the continued use of the army.

The peace that the army had imposed was only partial, for the IRA took advantage of the situation to resume its activities, basing itself, as in the 1920s, on the Roman Catholic area of Belfast. Right-wing unionists demanded stronger measures of repression; and in face of their criticisms Chichester-Clark resigned early in 1971. But his successor, Brian Faulkner, refused to be hurried into rash decisions, and continued his predecessor's policy, though with a greater appearance of activity. His main purpose was to restore confidence, both within the unionist party and among the population as a whole, while leaving the security forces to contain and wear down the resistance of the IRA. It was a purpose that had the full support of both major parties in Great Britain, and one that even the government of the republic, alarmed at the probable repercussions of continued violence in the north, could hardly wish to see fail.

By this time, however, the IRA had established itself too firmly in the Catholic districts of Belfast and Londonderry to be easily dislodged. From these bases it conducted a guerilla war, directed quite as much against the civilian population as against the army. Bomb attacks on public buildings, offices, shops, hotels and restaurants were made over a wide area; and, though some warning was generally given, the number of those killed or maimed, including many women and children, was considerable. Counter-attacks by extremist groups on the unionist side added to the general confusion. Extremists on both sides accused the army of brutality and of firing indiscriminately on hostile crowds; but politicians of all parties recognized that its presence was the only barrier against civil war; and as violence increased its role became more and more important. By March 1972 the British government (now once more in Conservative hands) had decided that, in this situation, responsibility for security should be transferred from the Northern Ireland cabinet to Whitehall. Rather than accept such a change, which it regarded as a surrender to anti-unionist political pressure, the Faulkner government resigned. In consequence, an act was hastily passed at Westminster suspending the Northern Ireland constitution and placing the province directly under the British government, with a secretary of state responsible for Northern Ireland affairs.

This measure was taken as the readiest means of getting round a difficulty; and the government in London probably regarded it as no more than a temporary expedient. Instead, it proved to be the end of an era, the final breakdown of the Irish settlement worked out in 1920–1 and confirmed by the governments of the United Kingdom, the Irish Free State and Northern Ireland in 1925. What new settlement is to take its place only the future can reveal.

Epilogue

The course of events since 1972 does not indicate any positive advance towards a general settlement. The entry of the United Kingdom and the Republic of Ireland into the European Economic Community in 1973 raised, in some quarters, a hope that within this larger framework an arrangement acceptable to all parties might be worked out; but this hope, never very realistic, was disappointed, and the problems that block the way to an enduring settlement of Irish affairs still remain.

These problems, though they appear in various forms, have a common root in the long-standing division within the population and the refusal of either side to recognize the need for a settlement acceptable to the other. During the 1960s such a recognition had seemed at last to be growing, however slowly; but the events of 1969–72 revived all the old antagonisms, and subsequent developments have done nothing to weaken them. The suspension of the Northern Ireland constitution in 1972 put the political future of the province in doubt; and it was natural that the government of the republic and public opinion both there and among Catholics in the north should see this as a step towards the incorporation of the six-county area in an all-Ireland state. It was equally natural that the northern protestants should feel that their position was now under threat and that they might find themselves placed, without their consent, under what they regarded as alien rule.

The extent and force of this fear among the protestant majority in Northern Ireland was revealed in 1974. The British government, though unwilling to restore the old constitution, was anxious to set up some form of devolved administration, in which the Roman Catholic minority was to have an assured place. A convention was elected on a system of proportional representation, which had been adopted to strengthen minority groups. The unionists, though they still had a clear majority of seats, were divided among themselves; and a substantial body of them agreed to combine with the Social and Democratic Labour party (SDLP), which represented the bulk of Catholic opinion, and with the newly founded Alliance party, to form an executive. Despite strong opposition from those more extreme unionists who had refused to co-operate, the executive functioned successfully for some months and seemed to be gaining support. But under pressure from Dublin and from the SDLP the British government insisted that this system of devolved administration should be accompanied by a 'Council of Ireland', in which the Northern Ireland executive and the government of the republic would co-operate; and the attempt to bring this council into being aroused all the traditional fears of the protestant population. A general strike, organized by an *ad hoc* body, the Ulster Workers' Council, brought economic life almost to a standstill; and in face of this reaction, even from their own supporters, the unionist members of the executive resigned. The strike ended at once; but a hopeful experiment in 'power-sharing' had ended in failure.

Though there can be no doubt that the strike was accompanied by a good deal of intimidation, its success was due to a general, if unjustified, fear among the protestant population as a whole that they were about to be handed over to the republic. It is significant that a later attempt to organize a similar strike over an issue in which relations with the republic were not involved failed completely.

The collapse of the executive left a political vacuum in Northern Ireland. But it had a positive result also; for it demonstrated that any solution to the 'Irish problem' must be found in Ireland itself and could not be imposed from Westminster. There is, however, no considerable group in any part of the country willing to accept the fact that a workable solution must be a compromise and that compromise involves, of necessity, a partial surrender of one's position. The government in Dublin expresses the hope that the majority in the north may change its mind and enter the republic willingly. But it has done nothing to induce such a change beyond removing from the constitution the section recognizing the special position of the Roman Catholic church; and since this gesture was regarded, even by the leaders of the church, as having no effect at all on the actual situation, it was unlikely to make much impression on the suspicious protestants of the north. To the latter, it seemed much more significant that the government of the republic urged the withdrawal of all British troops and that this course was supported by the Roman Catholic archbishop of Armagh. The Northern Ireland unionists, for their part, have shown little sympathy with the natural aspiration of the Catholic minority to strengthen links between north and south and to build up a framework within which a sense of common interest might develop.

Meanwhile, the IRA campaign continues, despite frequent condemnation by the ecclesiastical leaders and the elected representatives of the Catholic population on both sides of the border. The campaign has only strengthened the determination of the northern protestants not to allow themselves to be forced into the republic; but it has encouraged the growth, in Great Britain, of a popular opinion in favour of total withdrawal from Ireland. So far, however, both the major British political parties are committed to the principle that Northern Ireland should remain within the United Kingdom so long as a majority of the population wish it to do so; and, in fact, withdrawal against the wishes of the majority would create many problems for Britain and would put the government of the republic in a very difficult position. The British presence is not the cause but the result of division in Ireland; and it is hard to see how the division can be removed from the map until it has first been removed from the minds of men.

Guide to further reading

The following lists, which are intended mainly for the general reader and for those who are entering on the study of Irish history, contain only a small selection of the books available. Fuller information will be found in the bibliographies listed in section 1. It should be noted that titles included in sections 2–5 are not repeated in the later sections referring to particular periods.

1 Bibliographies

E. M. Johnston, *Irish history; a select bibliography*, rev. ed., London: Historical Association, 1972

Conyers Read, *Bibliography of British history: Tudor period*, rev. ed., Oxford, 1959

Godfrey Davis, *Bibliography of British history: Stuart period*, rev. ed., Oxford, 1971

S. M. Pargellis and D. J. Medley, *Bibliography of British history: the eighteenth century, 1714–89*, Oxford, 1951

'Writings on Irish history', published annually in *Irish Historical Studies*, Dublin, 1938–

Royal Historical Society, *Annual bibliography of British and Irish history*, London, 1976–

2 General works

E. Curtis, *History of Ireland*, 6th ed., London, 1960. The most substantial and most authoritative one-volume work.

B. Inglis, *The story of Ireland*, 2nd ed., London, 1968. A lively introduction to Irish history, with emphasis on the twentieth century.

T. W. Moody and F. X. Martin (eds.), *The course of Irish history*, Cork, 1967. A co-operative work, combining authority with popular appeal. Lavishly illustrated.

J. C. Beckett, *The making of modern Ireland, 1603–1923*, London and New York, 1966. Includes an introductory chapter on the Tudor period. Has a useful critical bibliography.

The Gill History of Ireland (Dublin, 1971–5) is a series of eleven volumes, each complete within its own area:
Gearoid MacNiocaill, *Ireland before the Vikings*
Donncha O Corrain, *Ireland before the Normans*
Michael Dolly, *Anglo-Norman Ireland*
Kenneth Nicholls, *Gaelic and Gaelicised Ireland in the middle ages*
John Watt, *The church in medieval Ireland*
James Lydon, *Ireland in the later middle ages*
Margaret MacCurtain, *Tudor and Stuart Ireland*
Edith M. Johnston, *Ireland in the eighteenth century*
Gearoid O Tuathaigh, *Ireland before the Famine, 1798–1848*
Joseph Lee, *The modernisation of Irish society, 1848–1914*
John A. Murphy, *Ireland in the twentieth century*

'A new history of Ireland', in nine volumes, edited by T. W. Moody, F. X. Martin and F. J. Byrne, is in course of publication. So far, only volume 3, *Early modern Ireland, 1534–1691* (Oxford, 1976), has appeared.

G. A. Hayes-McCoy, *Irish battles*, London, 1969. A history of warfare in Ireland by the leading authority on the subject.
T. W. Freeman, *Ireland: a general and regional geography*, 3rd ed., London, 1965
Ruth Dudley Edwards, *An atlas of Irish history*, London, 1973. Contains maps, with accompanying commentary, to illustrate the political, military, social and economic history of Ireland from the earliest times to the present day.

3   Ecclesiastical history

There is no satisfactory general work. The following are useful within the limits indicated by their titles:

W. A. Phillips (ed.), *History of the Church of Ireland*, 3 vols., Oxford, 1933–4
R. B. McDowell, *The Church of Ireland, 1869–1969*, London, 1975
P. J. Corish (ed.), *History of Irish Catholicism*, Dublin, 1967–71. Only a portion of this co-operative work has so far been published.

J. S. Reid, *History of the Presbyterian church in Ireland*, ed. W. D. Killen, 3 vols., Belfast, 1867

J. M. Barkley, *Short history of the Presbyterian church in Ireland*, Belfast 1959

H. C. Crookshank and R. Lee Cole, *History of Methodism in Ireland*, 4 vols., Belfast and London, 1885; 1960

4 Economic and social history

D. A. Akenson, *The Irish education experiment: the National system of education in the nineteenth century*, London, 1970

R. D. C. Black, *Economic thought and the Irish question, 1817–1870*, Cambridge, 1960. Examines the ideas that influenced government economic policy in Ireland during the nineteenth century.

J. C. Beckett and R. E. Glasscock (eds.), *Belfast: the origin and growth of an industrial city*, London, 1967

C. E. B. Brett, *Buildings of Belfast, 1700–1914*, London, 1967

R. A. Butlin (ed.), *The development of the Irish town*, London, 1977

G. Camblin, *The town in Ulster*, Belfast, 1951

D. A. Chart, *Ireland from the union to Catholic Emancipation*, London, 1910

D. A. Chart, *Economic history of Ireland*, Dublin, 1920. A brief but useful survey from pre-Norman times to the early twentieth century.

K. H. Connell, *The population of Ireland, 1750–1845*, Oxford, 1951

K. H. Connell, *Irish peasant society*, Oxford, 1966. Essays on rural life in the nineteenth and twentieth centuries.

J. C. Conroy, *History of railways in Ireland*, London, 1928

D. Corkery, *The hidden Ireland*, Dublin, 1925. A study of Gaelic Munster in the eighteenth century.

M. J. Craig, *Dublin, 1660–1860*, London, 1952. Mainly, but not exclusively, concerned with architecture.

L. M. Cullen, *Anglo-Irish trade, 1660–1800*, Manchester, 1968

L. M. Cullen, *Life in Ireland*, London, 1968. A very readable outline of Irish social history.

L. M. Cullen, *Economic history of Ireland since 1660*, London, 1972. The most authoritative work on the subject.

R. J. Dickson, *Ulster emigration to colonial America, 1750–1775*, London, 1968

J. S. Donnelly, *Landlord and tenant in nineteenth-century Ireland*, Dublin, 1973

T. W. Freeman, *Pre-Famine Ireland*, London, 1957. An admirable account of the state of the country in the early nineteenth century.

Conrad Gill, *The rise of the Irish linen industry*, Oxford, 1925: reprinted 1964

A. K. Longfield, *Anglo-Irish trade in the sixteenth century*, London, 1929

P. Lynch and J. Vaizey, *Guinness's brewery in the Irish economy, 1759–1876*, Cambridge, 1960

R. B. McDowell (ed.), *Social life in Ireland, 1800–1845*, Dublin, 1957

E. MacLysaght, *Irish life in the seventeenth century; after Cromwell*, 2nd ed., Cork, 1950

Mary McNeill, *Life and times of Mary Ann McCracken, 1770–1866: A Belfast panorama*, Dublin, 1960

Constantia Maxwell, *Dublin under the Georges, 1714–1830*, London, 1936

Constantia Maxwell, *Country and town in Ireland under the Georges*, 2nd ed., Dundalk, 1949

T. W. Moody and J. C. Beckett (ed.), *Ulster since 1800: a social survey*, London, 1957

A. E. Murray, *Commercial and financial relations between England and Ireland from the period of the Restoration*, London, 1903

G. O'Brien, *Economic history of Ireland in the seventeenth century*, Dublin, 1919

R. N. Salaman, *The social history of the potato*, Cambridge, 1949

Arthur Young, *Tour in Ireland*, ed. A. W. Hutton, 2 vols., London, 1892. Gives a contemporary view of rural Ireland, especially of its agriculture, in the later eighteenth century.

5 Collections of documents

E. Curtis and R. B. McDowell, *Irish historical documents, 1172–1922*, London, 1943

Constantia Maxwell, *Irish history from contemporary sources, 1509–1610*, London, 1929

H. Morley (ed.), *Ireland under Elizabeth and James I*, London, 1890. Contains works by Edmund Spenser, Sir John Davies and Fynes Moryson.

R. Dunlop, *Ireland under the Commonwealth*, 2 vols., Manchester, 1913. Selections from the state papers of the 1650s, with introduction and notes.

J. Carty, *Ireland from the Flight of the Earls to Grattan's Parliament*, Dublin, 1949

J. Carty, *Ireland from Grattan's Parliament to the Great Famine*, Dublin, 1949

J. Carty, *Ireland from the Great Famine to the Treaty*, Dublin, 1951. These three volumes contain, as well as documentary material of various kinds, many illustrations from contemporary sources.

W. H. Crawford and B. Trainor, *Aspects of Irish social history, 1750–1800*, Belfast, 1969

Patrick Buckland, *Irish unionism, 1885–1923: a documentary history*, Belfast, 1973

Education Facsimile Series, Public Record Office of Northern Ireland, Belfast. Sets of documents in facsimile, relating to particular topics or periods.

The Great Famine, 1845–52
Irish elections, 1750–1832
The Act of Union
The United Irishmen
The 1798 rebellion
The penal laws
Eighteenth-century Ulster emigration to North America
The Volunteers, 1778–84
Plantations in Ulster
Robert Emmet: the insurrection of July 1803
Steps to Partition, 1885–1921
Catholic Emancipation

6 Pre-Norman Ireland

Ludwig Bieler, *The life and legend of St Patrick*, Dublin, 1949
E. E. Evans, *Prehistoric and early Christian Ireland*, London, 1966
Kathleen Hughes, *The church in early Irish society*, London, 1966
R. A. S. Macalister, *Ancient Ireland*, London, 1935
R. A. S. Macalister, *The archaeology of Ireland*, 2nd ed., London, 1949
Eoin MacNeill, *Saint Patrick*, 2nd ed., Dublin and London, 1964,
T. F. O'Rahilly, *Early Irish history and mythology*, Dublin, 1946
J. Raftery, *Prehistoric Ireland*, London, 1951

7   Twelfth to fifteenth centuries

Olive Armstrong, *Edward Bruce's invasion of Ireland*, London, 1923

Donough Bryan, *The great earl of Kildare*, Dublin, 1933

E. Curtis, *A history of medieval Ireland*, 2nd ed., London, 1938

J. Lydon, *The lordship of Ireland*, Dublin, 1972

G. H. Orpen, *Ireland under the Normans, 1169–1333*, 4 vols., Oxford, 1911–20

A. J. Otway-Ruthven, *A history of medieval Ireland*, London, 1968

H. G. Richardson and G. O. Sayles, *The Irish parliament in the middle ages*, Philadelphia, 1952

H. G. Richardson and G. O. Sayles, *Parliament in medieval Ireland*, Dublin, 1964

G. T. Stokes, *Ireland and the Anglo-Norman church*, 3rd ed., London 1892

8   The Tudor period

R. Bagwell, *Ireland under the Tudors*, 3 vols., London, 1885–90

W. F. T. Butler, *Confiscation in Irish history*, 2nd ed., Dublin, 1918

R. Dudley Edwards, *Church and state in Tudor Ireland*, Dublin, 1935

Cyril Falls, *Elizabeth's Irish wars*, London, 1950

S. O. Faolain, *The Great O'Neill*, London, 1942

R. G. Morton, *Elizabethan Ireland*, London, 1971

D. B. Quinn, *The Elizabethans and the Irish*, New York, 1966

M. Ronan, *The Reformation in Ireland under Elizabeth*, London, 1930

P. Wilson, *The beginnings of modern Ireland*, London, 1912

9   The seventeenth century

R. Bagwell, *Ireland under the Stuarts*, 3 vols., 1909–16; reprint, London, 1963. A detailed narrative of the period 1603–90.

T. C. Barnard, *Cromwellian Ireland; English government and reform in Ireland, 1649–1660*, Oxford, 1975

Lady Brughclere, *Life of James, first duke of Ormonde*, 2 vols., London, 1912

Thomas Carte, *Life of James, first duke of Ormonde*, 3 vols., London, 1735–6. Ormond played a leading part in Irish politics from the 1630s to the 1680s. Carte's *Life* is mainly important for the large number of documents it contains.

Aidan Clarke, *The Old English in Ireland, 1625–1642*, London, 1966

D. Coffey, *O'Neill and Ormond*, Dublin, 1941

Hugh Kearney, *Strafford in Ireland, 1633–41*, Manchester, 1959

M. Perceval-Maxwell, *The Scottish migration to Ulster in the reign of James I*, London, 1973

T. W. Moody, *The Londonderry plantation, 1609–41*, Belfast, 1939

R. H. Murray, *Revolutionary Ireland and its settlement*, London, 1911

J. P. Prendergast, *The Cromwellian settlement of Ireland*, 3rd ed., Dublin, 1922

St John D. Seymour, *The Puritans in Ireland, 1647–61*, Oxford, 1921

J. G. Simms, *The Treaty of Limerick*, Dublin, 1961

J. G. Simms, *Jacobite Ireland, 1688–1691*, London, 1969

J. G. Simms, *The Williamite confiscation in Ireland, 1690–1703*, London, 1956

10 The eighteenth century

G. C. Bolton, *The passing of the Irish act of union*, Oxford, 1966

Albert Carré, *L'influence des Huguenots français en Irlande aux xviie et xviiie siècles*, Paris, 1937

M. J. Craig, *The Volunteer Earl*, London, 1948. A life of the first earl of Charlemont.

C. Litton Falkiner, *Studies in Irish history and biography*, London, 1902. Contains, among other items, essays on Grattan's parliament, Lord Clare and Lord Castlereagh.

O. W. Ferguson, *Jonathan Swift and Ireland*, Urbana, Illinois, 1962

J. A. Froude, *The English in Ireland in the eighteenth century*, new ed., 3 vols., London, 1881. Vividly written, but strongly marked by the author's own views.

Stephen Gwynn, *Henry Grattan and his times*, London, 1939

H. M. Hyde, *The rise of Castlereagh*, London, 1933

R. Jacob, *The rise of the United Irishmen*, London, 1937

F. G. James, *Ireland in the Empire, 1688–1770*, Cambridge, Mass., 1973

E. M. Johnston, *Great Britain and Ireland, 1760–1800: a study in political administration*, Edinburgh, 1963

L. A. Landa, *Swift and the Church of Ireland*, Oxford, 1954

W. E. H. Lecky, *History of Ireland in the eighteenth century*, new ed., 5 vols., London, 1912. The best general survey; but the first half of the century is treated only in outline. There is a useful abridgement of the whole work, with an introduction by L. P. Curtis, Chicago and London, 1972.

W. E. H. Lecky, *Leaders of public opinion in Ireland*, vol. 2, new ed., London, 1912. Studies of Flood and Grattan.

Grace L. Lee, *Huguenot settlements in Ireland*, London, 1936

F. MacDermot, *Theobald Wolfe Tone*, London, 1939

R. B. McDowell, *Irish public opinion, 1750–1800*, London, 1944

R. B. O'Brien (ed.), *Autobiography of Wolfe Tone*, 2 vols., London, 1893

M. R. O'Connell, *Irish politics and social conflict in the age of the American revolution*, Philadelphia, 1965

11   Nineteenth and twentieth centuries

F. S. L. Lyons, *Ireland since the Famine*, London, 1971. The fullest and most authoritative work covering the greater part of the period.

Robert Kee, *The green flag: a history of Irish nationalism*, London, 1972. After a brief introductory section concentrates on the period from 1798 onwards.

E. R. Norman, *A history of modern Ireland*, London, 1971. Begins with the parliamentary union.

O. MacDonagh, *Ireland: the union and its aftermath*, London, 1977. A brief but perceptive study of the effect of the union on political, economic and social life down to 1972.

D. P. Barritt and C. F. Carter, *The Northern Ireland problem*, London, 1962

P. Beaslai, *Michael Collins and the making of a new Ireland*, 2 vols., Dublin, 1926

D. G. Boyce, *Englishmen and Irish troubles: British public opinion and the making of Irish policy, 1918–22*, London, 1972

Patrick Buckland, *Irish unionism*, vol. 1: *The Anglo-Irish and the new Ireland, 1885–1922*, Dublin, 1972; vol. 2: *Ulster unionism and the origins of Northern Ireland, 1886–1922*, Dublin, 1973

Joseph T. Carroll, *Ireland in the war years, 1939–1945*, Newton Abbot and New York, 1975

M. Caulfield, *The Easter rebellion*, London, 1964

T. P. Coogan, *Ireland since the rising*, London, 1966

L. P. Curtis, *Coercion and conciliation in Ireland, 1880–92*, Princeton, 1963

L. P. Curtis, *Anglo-Saxons and Celts: A study in anti-Irish prejudice in Victorian England*, Connecticut, 1968

Michael Davitt, *The fall of feudalism in Ireland*, London, 1904

C. Gavan Duffy, *The league of north and south*, London, 1886

C. Gavan Duffy, *Thomas Davis*, London, 1890

R. D. Edwards and T. D. Williams (eds.), *The Great Famine: studies in Irish history, 1845–1852*, Dublin, 1956

St John Ervine, *Craigavon: Ulsterman*, London, 1949

Sir James Fergusson, *The Curragh incident*, London, 1963

Peter Gibbon, *The origins of Ulster unionism*, Manchester, 1975

Denis Gwynn, *The struggle for Catholic Emancipation*, London, 1928

Denis Gwynn, *Young Ireland and 1848*, Cork, 1949

J. L. Hammond, *Gladstone and the Irish nation*, London, 1938

D. W. Harkness, *The restless dominion: the Irish Free State and the British Commonwealth of Nations, 1921–31*, London, 1969

M. Harman (ed.), *Fenians and fenianism*, Dublin, 1968

R. M. Henry, *The evolution of Sinn Fein*, Dublin, 1920

M. W. Heslinga, *The Irish border as a cultural divide*, Assen, 1962

E. Holt, *Protest in arms: the story of the Irish troubles, 1916–1923*, London, 1960

H. M. Hyde, *Carson*, London, 1953

Brian Inglis, *Roger Casement*, London, 1973

Emmet Larkin, *James Larkin, Irish labour leader, 1876–1947*, London, 1965

Emmet Larkin, *The Roman Catholic church and the creation of the modern Irish state, 1878–1886*, Philadelphia and Dublin, 1975

R. J. Lawrence, *The government of Northern Ireland*, Oxford, 1965

W. E. H. Lecky, *Leaders of public opinion in Ireland*, vol. 2, new ed., London, 1912. A study of Daniel O'Connell.

Earl of Longford and T. P. O'Neill, *De Valera*, London, 1970

F. S. L. Lyons, *The Irish parliamentary party, 1890–1910*, London, 1951

F. S. L. Lyons, *The fall of Parnell*, London, 1960

F. S. L. Lyons, *John Dillon: a biography*, London, 1968

F. S. L. Lyons, *Parnell*, London, 1977

D. Macardle, *The Irish republic*, 4th ed., Dublin, 1951

J. L. McCracken, *Representative government in Ireland: Dáil Éireann, 1919–48*, Oxford, 1958

R. B. McDowell, *Public opinion and government policy in Ireland, 1801–1846*, London, 1952

R. B. McDowell, *The Irish administration, 1801–1914*, London, 1964

R. B. McDowell, *The Irish Convention, 1917–18*, London, 1970

A. Macintyre, *The Liberator: Daniel O'Connell and the Irish party, 1830–1847*, London, 1965

N. Mansergh, *The Irish question, 1840–1921*, London, 1965

N. Mansergh, *The Irish Free State, its government and politics*, London, 1934

N. Mansergh, *The government of Northern Ireland: a study in devolution*, London, 1936

E. Marjoribanks and I. Colvin, *Life of Lord Carson*, 3 vols., London, 1932–6

F. X. Martin (ed.), *Leaders and men of the Easter rising: Dublin, 1916*, London, 1967

D. W. Miller, *Church, state and nation in Ireland, 1898–1921*, Dublin, 1973

T. W. Moody (ed.), *The Fenian movement*, Cork, 1968

T. W. Moody and J. C. Beckett (ed.), *Ulster since 1800: a political and economic survey*, London, 1954

F. H. Newark *et al*, *Devolution of government, the experiment of Northern Ireland*, London, 1953

E. R. Norman, *The Catholic church and Ireland in the age of rebellion*, London, 1965

Index